Twayne's United States Authors Series

EDITOR OF THIS VOLUME

David J. Nordloh

Indiana University

Henry Adams

TUSAS 293

Henry Adams

HENRY ADAMS

By FERMAN BISHOP

Illinois State University

TWAYNE PUBLISHERS
A DIVISION OF G. K. HALL & CO., BOSTON

Published in 1979 by Twayne Publishers,
A Division of G. K. Hall & Co.
All Rights Reserved

Printed on permanent/durable acid-free paper and bound
in the United States of America

First Printing

Frontispiece photo of Henry Adams courtesy of the
Boston Public Library

Library of Congress Cataloging in Publication Data

Bishop, Ferman.
Henry Adams.

(Twayne's United States authors series; TUSAS 293)
Bibliography: p. 145–52
Includes index.
1. Adams, Henry, 1838–1918—Criticism and interpretation.
PS1004. A4Z6 818'.4'09 78-12060
ISBN 0-8057-7257-X

For Audrey

Contents

About the Author

Currently Professor of English at Illinois State University, Ferman Bishop has also taught at the Universities of Wisconsin, Colorado, and Wichita. He received his undergraduate degree from Wofford College as a William A. Law Scholar, and earned the Ph.D. degree from the University of Wisconsin with a doctoral dissertation on the mind and art of Sarah Orne Jewett. Professor Bishop's work on Jewett, Henry James, and Robert Frost has been published in *American Literature, Explicator,* and the *New England Quarterly.* In 1967, he published *Allen Tate* (TUSAS 124). Founder of the Midwest Modern Language Association, he served as its Secretary-Treasurer from 1959 through 1966. Now, in addition to lecturing in American literature, he is working on studies of William Gaddis and Saul Bellow.

Preface

The person seeking to become acquainted with Henry Adams will find himself provided with an abundance of materials: the number of books and articles about Adams reaches into the hundreds. But the problem of choosing a beginning has less to do with bulk than with substance; for Adams has attracted commentators of many different points of view, some of them diametrically opposed to each other. From the very beginning of his career, his political partisanship has had its defendants and opponents: his interpretation of Jefferson, for example, has always been controversial. Another of his interests, the problem of the relationship of science and history, has been the subject of voluminous discussion which has brought him both praise and blame. The question of whether or not Adams was a determinist has been debated. Still others have concerned themselves with his pessimism, though without unanimous agreement as to its cause. Perhaps this scholarly attention is a sign of Adams's vitality: dramatizing the urgency of some of the problems of men, he compels them to react.

This study attempts to prepare the reader to confront the Adams who is the focus of such twentieth-century controversy by providing him with a close examination of some of the minor essays and all of the major works. It seeks to present the historical context of Adams's works fully enough for the reader to place them in proper perspective. It follows a chronological sequence (with one exception) so that the reader can follow for himself the unfolding of a mind from its beginnings in journalism to its great discoveries of form in old age. The method of close reading allows stress to be placed on Adams's use of satire. Nearly everything Adams ever wrote had a satirical edge, and many of the mistakes in reading him have come from failure to understand his tone. More important, stress on his satire forces the reader to take into account Adams's entire mental perspective. Because the satirist is a moralist, he must believe in the ability of the human being to choose between alternative patterns of conduct; he cannot be the absolute determinist that Adams has sometimes been called. And if the satirist takes the trouble to try to induce people to choose, then he must be at least somewhat optimistic about their ability to choose aright; he cannot be the bleak pessimist that some have thought Adams to be. Adams was right in calling himself an eighteenth-century man, though even there he must have intended an irony. For like most Americans, he looked forward as well as backward, and it is the conflict between these two impulses that gives him such a rich sensibility.

In preparing this book, I have incurred more indebtedness than I can well acknowledge. I am grateful to Illinois State University for a sabbatical leave which enabled me to begin and for released time to continue the project. The staff of Milner Library at Illinois State University has assisted me in numerous ways, as has the staff of the University of Illinois Library. My wife has helped with many of the details of the study, particularly with the typing and preparation of the manuscript. And I wish especially to thank my editor, David J. Nordloh, who has been particularly helpful.

FERMAN BISHOP

Illinois State University

Chronology

1838 Henry Brooks Adams born February 16, in Boston, Massachusetts, the son of Charles Francis and Abigail Brooks Adams.

1850 Memorable trip to Washington, D.C., where he met President Taylor and visited Mount Vernon.

1854 Entered Harvard College.

1858 Arrived in Berlin, Germany, October 22, to begin study of Civil Law.

1859 Removal to Dresden; traveled in Germany, Austria, and Italy.

1860 Published letters in the *Boston Daily Courier;* returned to Quincy in October.

1860– Private secretary to his father, then a Congressman from
1861 Massachusetts, December-March; published "Letter from Washington" in the *Boston Daily Advertiser* from December through February.

1861– Private secretary to his father, who was Minister to Great
1868 Britain; wrote unsigned letters to the *New York Times*, 1861–1862; traveled to France, Denmark, Italy, and Germany.

1867 Published "Captain John Smith," "British Finance in 1816," and "The Bank of England Restriction," all in the *North American Review*.

1868 Review of the tenth edition of Sir Charles Lyell's *Principles of Geology* in the *North American Review*.

1868– Political journalist in Washington, D.C.; published articles
1870 in the *North American Review*, the *Edinburgh Review*, and the *Nation*.

1870 Published "The New York Gold Conspiracy" in the *Westminster Review;* traveled to England; appointed Assistant Professor of History at Harvard and Editor of the *North American Review*.

1871 Published, with his brother Charles Francis Adams, *Chapters of Erie, and Other Essays*.

1872 Married Marian Hooper, June 27.

1872– Wedding trip to Europe and Egypt.
1873

1876 Edited *Essays in Anglo-Saxon Law;* delivered the Lowell Lecture on "Primitive Rights of Women"; resigned the editorship of the *North American Review.*

1877 Resigned professorship at Harvard and moved to Washington, D.C.; published *Documents Relating to New England Federalism, 1800–1815.*

1879 Published *The Life of Albert Gallatin* and *The Writings of Albert Gallatin.*

1879– European trip to search archives for the *History of the United*
1880 *States during the Administrations of Thomas Jefferson and James Madison.*

1880 Published anonymously *Democracy: An American Novel.*

1882 Published *John Randolph* in the "American Statesmen" series.

1884 Published *Esther: A Novel* under the pseudonym Frances Snow Compton. Published privately *History of the United States of America During the First Administration of Thomas Jefferson.*

1885 Published privately *History of the United States of America During the Second Administration of Thomas Jefferson.* Suicide of Marian Hooper Adams, December 6.

1886 Tour of Japan with John La Farge.

1888 Published privately *History of the United States During the First Administration of James Madison.*

1889 Published *History of the United States During the First Administration of Thomas Jefferson.*

1890 Published *History of the United States During the Second Administration of Thomas Jefferson* and *History of the United States During the First Administration of James Madison.*

1891 Published *History of the United States During the Second*
1892 *Administration of James Madison* and *Historical Essays.*

1890– Traveled with John La Farge to Hawaii, Samoa, Tahiti, Fiji,
1892 Australia, Ceylon, Grance, and England.

1892– Made almost yearly trips to Europe, commonly spending
1914 seven months of each year in Paris.

1893 Published privately *Memoirs of Marau Taaroa, Last Queen of Tahiti.*

Chronology

1894   Published "The Tendency of History," an essay composed as his Presidential Address to the American Historical Association.

1904   *Mont-Saint-Michel and Chartres* privately printed.

1907   *The Education of Henry Adams* privately printed.

1908   Edited *Letters of John Hay and Extracts from Diary.*

1910   Published *A Letter to American Teachers of History.*

1911   Published *The Life of George Cabot Lodge.*

1912   Suffered cerebral thrombosis, April 24.

1913   *Mont-Saint-Michel and Chartres* published under the sponsorship of the American Institute of Architects.

1918   Died in Washington, D.C., March 27; publication of *The Education of Henry Adams* by the Massachusetts Historical Society.

1919   Brooks Adams edited and published *The Degradation of the Democratic Dogma.*

1920   Mabel La Farge edited and published *Letters to a Niece and Prayer to the Virgin of Chartres.*

CHAPTER 1

The Formative Years

B Y the time of the birth of Henry Adams, his family had been a prominent part of the American scene for nearly two hundred years. The weight of the responsibility of this heritage bore heavily upon each new member of the family, as Henry reflected in the famous passage about his own birth in his *Education:* "Had he been born in Jerusalem under the shadow of the Temple and circumcized in the Synagogue by his uncle the high priest, under the name of Samuel Cohen, he would scarcely have been more distinctly branded, and not much more handicapped in the races of the coming century, in running for such stakes as the century had to offer."[1] In spite of the irony, Adams obviously enjoyed responding to the challenge of living in the reflected light of his famous forebears. So much did he identify himself with them that nearly everything he ever wrote shows the impress of their character.

I *The Adams Heritage*

The Adams fame had not come from any gradual accumulation of resources: it came suddenly into focus in the person of John Adams. The family had never shown any inclination to leadership, either in England or in America.[2] The single circumstance which gave the Adams family its start toward international prominence was the passage of the Stamp Act in 1765.[3] John Adams took a stand against the English position and argued so capably that he quickly established his reputation as a thinker on constitutional law. Later, he served on the committee of the Continental Congress for framing the Declaration of Independence. He helped to draw up the treaty of peace with Great Britain, and he served as the first American minister to England. In 1789 he became the country's first Vice-President, and in 1797, its second President. Defeated for reelection by Thomas Jefferson in 1800, he retired to private life.

15

His son, John Quincy Adams, began his indoctrination into the responsibilities of public life at the age of eleven, when he accompanied his father on a diplomatic mission to France.[4] Thereafter to the end of his life he was, with only a few exceptions, continuously in the public service. He was successively Minister to the Netherlands, United States Senator, Minister to Russia, and Secretary of State. In this last capacity he negotiated the treaty which gave the United States possession of Florida, and he did the essential work required before the promulgation of the Monroe Doctrine. He served as President from 1825 through 1829, rather unsuccessfully because of the opposition of the Jacksonians. In the year after his retirement he was elected to Congress, where he worked actively against the extension of slavery almost to the day of his death, February 23, 1848.

Charles Francis Adams, the son of John Quincy Adams and father of Henry Adams, like his father received an early exposure to the public service.[5] But he devoted much of his attention to business. He served in both the Massachusetts House and in the Senate. He was elected to the United States Congress in 1859. His greatest opportunity came when Lincoln appointed him Minister to Great Britain in 1861. Taking along his son Henry as private secretary, he successfully carried out his diplomatic mission, which had as its main purpose the maintenance of English neutrality. Despite the high level of ability and dedication he showed on this mission, the country, then under the control of the Grant administration, could find no position for him. This repudiation of his father was one of the causes of Henry's disillusionment with post–Civil War politics in America.

James Truslow Adams observes that no other family in America has been able to elevate itself to a place of such prominence over so long a period of time.[6] Whatever the mechanism of their transmission of the heritage, it had suffered no diminution as it reached the fourth generation in Henry Adams. Even as a child in church he had opportunity to see that his grandfather and great-grandfather were prominent men. And in old age he remembered his shock as a boy that the gardener should doubt that he was destined to be President.[7] Long before he went to school, he had acquired the habit of looking at himself as an object of the Adams heritage, a fact which had its privileges but also its responsibilities.

II *Education, 1848–1858*

One of the most famous scenes in the *Education* begins with a picture of a recalcitrant young Henry Adams, who refused to go to school one summer morning.[8] Nothing that his mother said availed to change his mind. But then old John Quincy Adams emerged from his study, placed a hat on his head, and took the boy by the hand. Without a word the old man escorted his grandson to school. The boy knew how many important matters the old Congressman had on his mind, and even a child could understand the dignity of silence. After a lesson so replete with symbolism, little wonder that so much education afterwards paled in his imagination!

Adams always deprecated formal education, probably not so much from dislike of schooling as from its always falling short of the demands his idealism put upon it. In the *Education* he omitted entirely any mention of his attendance at Tower's school, and he wrote only of his relief at leaving Dixwell's.[9] He seemed to take especial delight in deprecating his training at Harvard. He accused the college of failing to introduce him to the two thinkers most needful for him to know—Karl Marx and Auguste Comte. In order to cope with the world ahead of him he needed four subjects— mathematics, French, German, and Spanish—but he never mastered any one of them. Although he admitted that Louis Agassiz and James Russell Lowell had given him superior instruction, he summarized the general effect of the college by saying that it "taught little, and that little ill, but it left the mind open, free from bias, ignorant of facts, but docile."[10] The work of his four years at Harvard, he said, could have been accomplished in four months at the speed he later attained. The college had to be reckoned a negative force.

The research of Ernest Samuels into Adams's Harvard career tends to show otherwise.[11] If Adams did not receive all the training in modern languages that he wished, he did read widely in the classics. In Greek he studied the *Odyssey*, Euripides' *Alcestis*, Isocrates' *Panegyrics*, Sophocles' *Ajax* and *Oedipus Tyrannus*. In Latin he read Livy, Cicero's *Tusculan Disputations* and *Brutus*, Horaces's *Odes* and *Satires*, Tacitus' *Annals*, and Quintillian's *Institutes*. In mathematics he worked at a comparatively low level: beginning with plane geometry, he also studied solid geometry, trigonometry, algebra, and analytic geometry. In his courses in history he studied Thomas Arnold's *Lectures on Modern History,* Robertson's *View of the Progress of Society in Europe from the Subversion of the Roman Empire to the Beginning of the Sixteenth Century,* and Guizot's *History of the Origin of Representative Government in Europe.* In addition, he took courses in the sciences, ethics, political economy, and rhetoric.

Adams's true rank as a scholar at Harvard was distorted by the "Scale of Merit" grading system then in effect.[12] Position on the "Scale of Merit" was determined mathematically, with points being assigned for recitations, papers, declamations, and other academic exercises; but subtractions were made for such infractions of the rules as tardiness at prayers, smoking, or shouting to someone from an upstairs window. Adams incurred so many subtractions that his high standing in academic subjects did not show; on the "Scale of Merit" his rating was only mediocre. But his abilities must have impressed his classmates, for they elected him Class Day Orator. And some years later his academic record did not deter President Eliot from appointing him to the Harvard faculty.

III   *European Tour*

In the autobiographical sketch that he wrote for the "Life Book" of the Class of 1858, Adams wrote of his ambition to study in Europe.[13] Some of his enthusiasm may have come from his association with James Russell Lowell, who had returned to America in 1856 after a year spent mostly in Germany. Adams wrote of his ambition to increase his command of languages, and he also mentioned his desire to study law as three generations of Adamses before him had done. In the autumn he sailed for Germany, where he planned to study civil law at the University of Berlin. His choice would have pleased John Adams himself, who had recommended that a young lawyer study civil law in the original tongues.[14] And Berlin had one of the most prestigious centers in the world for the study of civil law.

When Adams arrived in Berlin on October 22, he found the term already under way.[15] But he also discovered that he understood too little German to cope with lectures in the university. He tried to solve the problem by enrolling in a gymnasium, where he could study Latin and Greek and practice German with boys who could speak no English. He made only indifferent progress in his studies, but he used his free time to attend musical and dramatic performances. At the end of the term he left Berlin for Dresden.[16] He dropped all pretense of studying civil law. For much of the remainder of his two years in Europe he was simply a tourist. In the spring and summer he traveled in Germany, Belgium, Holland, Italy, and France; in the winter he studied German and did desultory reading in Dresden.

Of all the experiences during his grand tour of Europe, the one of greatest significance for Adams's development was one which took place at the church of Santa Maria di Ara Coeli in Rome.[17] He went there, a Murray's guidebook in hand, on an evening in May 1860. Near this spot, in October 1764, Gibbon had observed monks singing vespers in the ruins of the Temple of Jupiter. Struck by the irony of their seeming mockery of the greatest temple of the Romans, Gibbon conceived on the spot the idea of writing *The Decline and Fall of the Roman Empire*. For Adams, who came to think of Gibbon as the greatest historian in English, the dramatic force of the scene must have been overwhelming.

In the *Education*, Adams suggests the pivotal importance of this episode for his own development, returning to it again and again as a point of reference. But his rendition is very different from that of Gibbon. The English historian's eye fell upon the Roman ruins; for him the irony of the scene arose from the triumph of an effeminate Christianity over a more deserving Rome. Adams did not mention the Roman ruins at all; instead he concentrated on the picture of the steps and the name of the church, in English, "Altar of Heaven." The symbolism of the 122 marble steps leading up to the repose of the old church, a place of order contrasting sharply with the chaos all around, would have been congenial to the later Adams. How much he understood at twenty-two might be open to conjecture, but his seeking out the locale bespoke a certain sensitivity to the symbols of history.

IV *The Great Secession Winter*

When Adams returned to America in the fall of 1860, he began reading law with Judge Horace Gray.[18] He was soon summoned to Washington to assist his father, who was striving from his position as Congressman to find a compromise that would preserve the Union. While acting as secretary to his father, Henry Adams wrote a series of articles on political subjects for the *Boston Daily Advertiser*. He also wrote a comprehensive essay, "The Great Secession Winter,"

which he intended to publish.[19] But he decided it was not worth
printing, and it did not appear until 1910, in the *Proceedings* of the
Massachusetts Historical Society.

The sketch is especially interesting for its authorial stance, in
which a youthful Henry Adams writes with far less detachment than
he would permit himself in his later works.[20] His interpretation
from the viewpoint of the moderate Republicans caused him to
attribute hysteria or villainy to the opposition. He was especially
hard on Breckenridge, one of the defeated candidates for the Presidency in 1860; Adams declared that he was part of "a wide-spread
and intricate conspiracy" to seize the government in Washington.[21]
Although Senator Douglas had discovered the conspiracy and had
labored to defeat it, he did not receive Adams's entire approbation,
because he had done more than anyone else "to degrade the standard of political morality and to further the efforts of the slave
power."[22] Adams did find two men who deserved admiration—An-
drew Johnson of Tennessee and Henry Winter Davis of Maryland,
both of whom worked strongly for the preservation of the Union.
Adams concluded on a hopeful note: he saw the "slave power," the
force which had subverted the entire country, now defeated fairly in
the election of 1860. No other government could have extirpated
such a power without great bloodshed. Adams was still hopeful that
the great secession winter, "the first crucial test of our political
system,"[23] would end peacefully, even though the President had
already called for arms.

CHAPTER 2

The Making of a Historian

IN March 1861, Henry Adams returned to Boston to begin reading law once more in the office of Judge Gray.[1] Only a few days later Lincoln appointed his father, Charles Francis Adams, Minister to Great Britain. Because of the importance of the post, the senior Adams decided that Henry must once again serve as his private secretary. An influential segment of English society was wavering toward recognition of the Confederacy, an action which would do great harm to the military stance of the United States. Because of the delicate diplomatic situation, the Minister would need all his energies to concentrate on negotiations at the highest level. The urgency of the situation became clear at the moment of the new Minister's landing in England, when he heard that Her Majesty's government had issued the Proclamation of Neutrality, which in effect recognized Confederate belligerency. In all the strain about the legation, the private secretary was supposed to function quietly, overseeing routine duties so as to free the Minister for diplomacy.

But Henry Adams was not one to be passive. Before going to England, he arranged, without his father's knowledge, to serve as correspondent for the *New York Times*.[2] This arrangement provided the Minister with sympathetic coverage in the American press and protected him from possible embarrassment. Incidentally it enabled Henry to continue his development as a writer. This arrangement functioned smoothly until a special story placed by his brother Charles with the *Boston Courier* carried Henry's name.[3] The story did not compromise anything; it was merely a witty comparison of social events in Manchester and London. But the American editor's indiscretion brought Henry to the attention of the London *Times* and jeopardized his father's position. The tempest soon subsided with no harm done except to Henry's aspirations as a writer. Thoroughly upset, he severed his connection with the *New York*

21

Times and henceforth concentrated on his duties as private secretary.

I *Intellectual and Social Life in London*

Although Adams cultivated the pose of obscure private secretary, he was obviously well aware of his own ability to profit from the social and intellectual life of London. The legation attracted an enormous number of the most stimulating thinkers in Victorian England.[4] Among those who called during the Adams tenure were Robert Browning, Sir Charles Lyell, John Bright, Thomas Baring, and James Anthony Froude. On one occasion Adams dined in the company of Charles Dickens, and on another he discussed free trade with John Stuart Mill. His friend Charles Milnes Gaskell introduced him to Francis Turner Palgrave, editor of *The Golden Treasury*. His taste, Adams said, gave him "more literary education than he ever got from any taste of his own."[5] Gaskell also introduced Adams to Algernon Swinburne, whose genius both impressed Adams and made him feel inadequate.[6]

For the mental development of the historian the ferment of ideas in London must have meant as much as the casual acquaintance of the great. Darwin's *Origin of Species* had been published only a few years before; its implications for history, and particularly religious history, had already produced heated debate. Adams became well acquainted with Sir Charles Lyell, who professed to be a Darwinian.[7] Lyell's book *The Antiquity of Man* was published in 1863 to bolster the position of the scientists who wished to demonstrate principles of development in human as well as in plant and animal life. Adams, too, called himself a Darwinian, though with reservations. At Harvard he had studied under Louis Agassiz, who had pioneered in the study of glaciation and whose observations led him to stress cataclysmic change as the most important principle for the interpretation of the history of the earth. He regarded the Darwinians as intellectual opposites who overstressed the idea of uniformitarian change. Adams found merit in both positions, but he had difficulty reconciling the two. In his discussions with Lyell about the principles of change, Adams convinced the geologist of the need for allowing more stress on the phenomena of glaciation. Lyell was evidently impressed, for he later asked Adams to review the tenth edition of his *Principles of Geology*.[8] Though still appreciative of Lyell's powers of observation and reasoning, Adams showed that he still felt uncomfortable in trying to reconcile the arguments for cataclysmic and uniformitarian development. Unable to declare himself for evolution, he declared in the *Education* that "all he could prove was change."[9]

He found the theories of Auguste Comte about the principles of change in human history more to his liking. Discovering the popularization *Auguste Comte and Positivism* by John Stuart Mill as soon as it was published in 1865, Adams soon regarded himself a disciple of Comte.[10] The most congenial part of Comte's thought was his explanation of the movement of thought.[11] He believed that man first goes through a theological stage, in which he conceives of the universe as responding to the wills of real or imaginary beings. After this attitude is exhausted, there arises the metaphysical stage, in which god or gods are discarded in favor of abstractions, the chief of which is the concept of Nature. After a time this attitude passes over into the positive stage, in which it is recognized that natural causes, not supernatural, lie behind every phenomenon in the universe. Adams seems to have accepted these generalizations readily enough, probably because they were large enough to be suggestive rather than confining. Yet it would be a mistake to believe that he accepted all of Comte. He was far too skeptical to become a disciple of anyone, particularly of the Comte who elevated positivism to a religion.

The patterns of history occupied many another thinker in Victorian England, and Adams would have been hard put to avoid most of them. He had been an admirer of Carlyle[12] and would continue to use his ideas even as late as the *Education*, though their attitudes toward the Civil War seem to have kept them apart. In England Adams became interested in the thought of Henry Buckle,[13] who advocated the application to history of the ideas of science. He assimilated Herbert Spencer's generalizations about evolution.[14] In sum, Adams showed in his contacts with Victorian intellectuals that he, like so many of them, was quickened by the problems of history. The questions raised during his stay in London must have helped to shape the attitudes of his adult life, though some of his answers were not formulated until his old age.

II   *The Earliest History, "Captain John Smith"*

Adams's first historical research stemmed from a suggestion of John Gorham Palfrey, the Massachusetts historian.[15] During a visit to the Adams house in the spring of 1861, he mentioned that the Pocahontas story would make an interesting investigation. It was especially interesting because some of the Virginia families traced their ancestry to Pocahontas; if her story proved doubtful, the investigator would at least have an intellectual victory for the Union. Henry Adams liked the idea well enough to begin research in the British Museum shortly after he took up his duties at the legation in London. At first he thought the results unpromising. He wrote on October 23, 1861, to Palfrey, explaining his reasons for thinking that the commonly accepted version of the story might be right after all. Palfrey referred his letter to Charles Deane, who made several suggestions for improving Adams's research. Though Adams soon reported to Palfrey that he was once again working on the project,[16] he delayed more than four years in sending off the final manuscript to the *North American Review*, where it was published in January 1867.

Adams's article took the form of a review of two books edited by Charles Deane: *A Discourse of Virginia* by Edward Maria Wingfield and *A True Relation of Virginia* by Captain John Smith.[17] The article was essentially an elaboration of the thesis laid down by Deane: the failure of Captain John Smith to write about his rescue by Pocahontas in the early *True Relation* suggests that the story is a fabrication. (More recently, Grace Steele Woodward has remarked that no one has explained this omission, but she believes that Smith may have been trying to conceal from prospective colonists the danger from the Indians.[18]) In Adams's view, however, Smith's handling of the story is of a piece with the rest of his character, which Adams interprets unfavorably.

His technique foreshadows some of his later writing, particularly the *Life of Albert Gallatin*. Placing quotations from Smith's *A True Relation* of 1608 side by side with corresponding passages from *The Generall Historie* of 1624, he italicizes the discrepancies in Smith's story.[19] The later narrative, he demonstrates, has a "curious tone of exaggeration." Eight guards in the 1608 version become thirty or forty in 1624. Four guides are increased to twelve. The Indians in the earlier version are kind and hospitable; later they are ferocious. In the earlier version Pocahontas is not mentioned at all, whereas in 1624 she is the means of Smith's salvation. Adams then examines other narratives that might have been likely to mention Smith's rescue. One, the Oxford tract of 1612 apparently written by Smith, mentions Pocahontas as his guardian angel, but it does not describe her most famous act. William Strachey's manuscript of about 1615 mentions Pocahontas, but not the rescue. Ralphe Hamor's book of 1615 mentions her marriage and describes her political importance, but does not mention her saving Captain Smith. Purchas writes about her trip to England and her death in 1617 but does not include the rescue. Only after the death of Pocahontas and of Queen Anne in 1619 did Smith bring out the famous story. Adams confesses that the acceptance of Smith's story at the time of its publication and its persistence beyond that date were for him puzzles difficult to explain.

Perhaps the most interesting aspect of this early essay is not its careful use of evidence, though this is important in its anticipation of the "scientific" elements in Adams's history. More important still was his attempt to confront and explain the mythical element in history. He confessed that he could see but could not fathom the strong attraction which Smith exerted on Pocahontas. His struggle with the material for five years before submitting it for publication suggests the difficulty he had in resolving the story in his own mind. His final acknowledgment of the power of the story, though phrased with irony, hints that the story has life greater than mere rationality can explain and that this life may not have been obliterated even by the power of his own scholarship.

Adams's interest in the story came in part from the same impulse that caused him to pause at Santa Maria di Ara Coeli. He was drawn by its symbolic qualities, even though he did not have the technical equipment for their analysis. If he had had the benefit of an understanding of mythical criticism, he would have seen that Pocahontas represents the primitive, passive, and undefiled side of the human condition, whereas John Smith stands for the civilized, aggressive, and sophisticated. The appeal of the story lies in its ability to create a myth which resolves these forces in such a way as to satisfy our desire for the triumph of the right. The spiritual power of woman to insure that goodness should prevail over evil was a theme to which Adams would return: Pocahontas is the precursor of Madeleine Lee, the Tahitian women, and especially the Virgin of Chartres.

III *Reform Journalism: "The New York Gold Conspiracy"*

When Henry Adams returned to America in July 1868, he found the tone of the nation very different from that he had known seven years earlier.[20] The passions of Reconstruction had the country so firmly in their grip that the eighteenth-century reasonableness of an Adams seemed a complete anachronism. Even his old friend Charles Sumner, now powerful in the Senate, was now alienated from their influence. But what might be bad for government could be turned to account for drama. Henry saw the possibilities for journalism and removed to Washington to be near his primary materials. His numerous connections opened many doors for him, even those of the White House, where he met President Johnson. Soon he was contributing to such famous journals as the *Nation,* the *Edinburgh Review,* and the *North American Review.* He was especially interested in reform: for him a return to the high standards of personal honesty and dedication of John Quincy Adams would have been exactly what the post–Civil War government needed.

Like most of his countrymen, Adams voted for Grant for President in 1868. The General seemed a force for law and order, but Adams was soon disillusioned with his choice. Even before Grant's inauguration, the drift of his administration was all too clearly signaled by the quality of the appointments to his cabinet. Adams lamented in a letter to Charles Milnes Gaskell, "My hopes of the new administration have all been disappointed: it is far inferior to the last. My friends have all lost ground instead of gaining it as I hoped. My family is buried politically beyond recovery for years."[21] Adams's evaluation was soon proved accurate: not only was the new administration weak, it was corrupt as well. One of the most spectacular bits of scandal was the attempt by Jay Gould and James Fisk, Jr., to establish a corner in the gold market. Adams, who knew that manipulation of gold prices required the cooperation of highly placed officers in the Executive branch, watched the excitement and the subsequent congressional investigation with the most intense interest. Long afterward, he wrote in the *Education* that he expected to find Grant himself implicated.[22] Perhaps it was this possibility that made Adams determine to write an account of the scandal. He did his research with enthusiasm: to the materials brought out by the congressional hearing, headed by James A. Garfield, he added what he was able to glean from other sources.[23] When the story was finished, he realized that he could not publish it in America for fear of lawsuits for libel. Even in England he did not succeed in placing it in the *Quarterly Review,* as he had wished; instead it appeared in the *Westminster Review* for October 1870.

"The New York Gold Conspiracy" is the best piece of writing Adams had done up to that time; it shows an imagination fully engaged and in control of its materials. The writer is a moralist, a satirist taking his tone from an idealistic interpretation of government that would have suited John Quincy Adams. His choice of form is superb: he tells his story through an impersonal narrator, who only once or twice descends to the first-personal plural. He quickly takes up a stance far above the subjects of his story so that they all, from the President of the United States down to the humblest citizen, take on Lilliputian dimensions. In particular, Adams castigates the sin of avarice, which he sees as rampant from the period of the Civil War onward. A "speculative mania" gripped the entire group of Northern states during that time, so that "every farmer and every shopkeeper in the country seemed to be engaged in 'carrying' some favorite security 'on a Margin.' "[24] As long as the currency was being inflated, the speculators prospered. But the drastic deflation after the Civil War caught many of them unaware, so that losses were almost universal. Adams interprets this governmental policy as a "return to solid values"[25] and paints the losses as retribution: "Some men, who had courage and a sense of honor, found life too heavy for them; others went mad. But the greater turned in silence to their regular pursuits, and accepted their losses as they could."[26] These introductory pictures have less to do with Adams's narrative than with his establishment of a satiric norm. Adams is seeking to gain his reader's identification with a moral point of view that elevates the rational and ridicules the follies brought about by the passions of mankind.

Adams's narrative proper begins with the ascendancy of Jay Gould and James Fisk, Jr., over the Erie Railroad in July 1868, a deed accomplished without nicety of moral scruple. Gould, Adams says, was given to silent intrigue: "He spun huge webs, in corners and in the dark, which were seldom strong enough to resist a serious strain at the critical moment."[27] His partner, Fisk, was equally ludicrous: he "was not yet forty years of age, and had the instincts of fourteen."[28] As to the problem of the relative dishonesty of each man, Adams finally awards the palm to Fisk, "who seldom or never speaks the truth at all."[29]

The ostentatious habits which Fisk and Gould brought to the headquarters of the Erie bring out some of Adams's sharpest satire: "The suite of apartments was then furnished by themselves, as rep-

resenting the corporation, at an expense of some $60,000, and in a
style which, though called vulgar, is certainly not more vulgar than
that of the President's official residence, and which would be
magnificent in almost any palace in Europe."[30] The expense of
maintaining such an establishment placed a severe strain on even
the Erie Railroad, but the partners had resources denied to men of
scruple. They made enormous sums by selling short the stock of an
express company which had a contract with the Erie. They announced the cancellation of the contract, at which time the stock of
the express company fell. The partners covered their short sales,
made new purchases of stock, and then announced the renewal of
the contract. In 1869 they sold new stock in the Erie equal to the
entire valuation of the company when they assumed control in 1868.
Adams comments: "The process was different from that known to
the dark ages, but the objects and the results were equally robbery."[31]

The scheme which next entered Gould's imagination—that of
cornering the American gold market—may have fascinated him
even more for its danger than for its ability to produce money.
Adams comments with obvious irony: "His fertile mind even went
so far as to discover that it would prove a blessing to the community,
and on this ingenious theory, half honest and half fraudulent, he
stretched the widely extended fabric of the web in which all mankind was to be caught."[32] Gould had no problem finding funds to
drive the price of gold up, but he did have to insure himself against
the intervention of the federal government. He enlisted the cupid-
ity of the President's brother-in-law, Abel Rathbone Corbin, who
was expected to influence Grant in favor of the conspirators.

Some of Adams's sharpest satire was directed at Grant himself.
He was elaborately entertained by Fisk and Gould at the headquarters of the Erie, and then accepted an invitation to their yacht,
where Fisk was dressed "in a blue uniform, with a broad gilt cap-
band, three silver stars on his coat-sleeve, lavender gloves, and a
diamond breast-pin as large as a cherry."[33] If Grant could take this
display seriously, it was little wonder that Corbin could sway him to
Gould's theory of the need for a higher price for gold. Grant's letter
of instruction to the Secretary of the Treasury was dated September
4, 1869;[34] by that time Corbin himself was a heavy purchaser of
gold.

Grant's seeming obliviousness to intrigue continued even after the battle between the bulls and the bears grew furious. The huge speculative purchases and sales of gold brought the financial business of the country to a standstill. Finally the President heard about Corbin's speculation and forced him out of the market. With the government swinging to the opposite side, Gould's scheme collapsed. Gold fell from 160 to 135 in fifteen minutes, and when the government confirmed its willingness to sell at that figure, there was no possibility of recovery.

In a long concluding paragraph, Adams writes a little essay on the problems of power in modern political life. The Gold Conspiracy, he says, will prove good for the United States because the people will demand reform. The country, he feels sure, will abandon its experiments with paper money and act to curb speculation. But he is less optimistic about the more distant future. The corporation has demonstrated that it can place enormous power in the hands of a few men, so much that it may be difficult for the government itself to control. And if the government is forced to become powerful enough to control men of the stamp of Gould or Fisk, then it may be too fearsome an instrument for the safety of the people.

Adams might well have followed up on the success of "The New York Gold Conspiracy" with other articles of the kind; certainly the Grant era provided no dearth of materials for the satirist bent on reform. In more than a dozen political essays, Adams demonstrated his command of the Washington scene. One of his essays was printed for national distribution by the Democratic party. But when he went to Europe for a summer vacation in 1870, he did not return to Washington, and his career in journalism was over. Why? Perhaps the clue to Adams's seeming fickleness lay in the mind of President Grant. As the *Education* reported many years later, Adams saw that Grant was too unbelievably simpleminded to be the product of a complex civilization. Adams quipped that "the progress of evolution from President Washington to President Grant, was alone evidence enough to upset Darwin."[35] Yet his wit masked his feeling of insecurity in the presence of Grant's banalities. Followers of such a man could only relegate an Adams to the opposition, a stance that could be interesting only if one were sparring with his equals. Because few in the Grant administration had the capability of an Adams, Henry was forced to seek other fields.

IV   *Professor and Editor at Harvard*

During the spring before he left for Europe Adams had been offered the editorship of the *North American Review*, the prestigious journal in which he had been publishing regularly.[36] He declined, saying that he wished to continue his career in political journalism. Then in July President Eliot of Harvard offered him an assistant professorship of history. Again Adams declined. When he arrived back in Boston he found the Harvard offer renewed, and this time under the prodding of his family he accepted. His contract called for him both to teach medieval history and to edit the *North American Review*. His credentials for the post seemed most slender: he had ranked only in the middle of his class as an undergraduate and he had no graduate work to his credit. President Eliot had evidently put his estimate of the man ahead of academic qualifications. Adams's writing showed him the brilliance of his scholarship; it mattered little that he had not written on the subject he was to teach.

Although Adams in the *Education* deprecated his own ability to profit from his teaching at Harvard,[37] he could not have been writing about the amount of learning he absorbed from his preparations. Sometimes he went frantically through four books a day, as well he might in presenting the history of Europe from the tenth through the seventeenth century. Although he joked about his own inability to pass the examinations he gave, the demands he made of his students could not have been as great as those he imposed on himself. Most taxing of all were the seminars he gave for doctoral candidates in the last three years of his tenure.[38] Adams was one of the early, though not the earliest, users of this method of instruction in America. Like the Germans from whom they had taken the method, Adams and his students went back to the original sources in their search for answers to the problems they had set themselves. Adams's first seminar resulted in a book on Anglo-Saxon law, in which the first essay, "The Anglo-Saxon Courts of Law," by the professor himself preceded three others by his students.

In his introductory essay to the work of his doctoral candidates, Adams wrote a more technical exposition of a problem in history than he ever before had done or would ever do again. He paid homage to the labors of the German scholars whose methods he was emulating, giving them credit for establishing the most important principle of historical scholarship of recent years.[39] They had discovered that the foundations of democracy had been established in the social organization of the ancient Germanic tribes and that this heritage had been transmitted in a direct line to their descendants. This thesis, though now discredited, gave Adams and his students emotional justification for their efforts to establish the nature of Anglo-Saxon law.

Adams's problem was to describe and interpret the function of the Anglo-Saxon courts of law. He was convinced that they closely paralleled their counterparts in Germany, where "there was but one political or judicial subdivision of the state, . . . the district, known commonly as the hundred."[40] In this interpretation he differed strongly from Edward A. Freeman, the famous English historian of the Norman Conquest of England, who believed that the shire was an aggregation of marks and the kingdom an aggregation of shires. To disprove Freeman's thesis, Adams found it necessary to prove the existence of the district, or hundred, as a political subdivision from the earliest times.[41] To do so, he cited seven examples of early Anglo-Saxon texts which mentioned the existence of the hundred. From this evidence Adams concluded that the hundred was the only political subdivision of the early Anglo-Saxons and that its court was therefore their most important governmental assembly, just as it was for their kinsmen among the primitive Germans. By the time of Alfred there were three courts, the hundred, the shire, and the *Witan*, but each of them was an adaptation of the primitive popular assembly. The Anglo-Saxon king, he pointed out, was never considered an originator of justice because he had no powers separate from those of the court in which he sat. The Anglo-Saxons, like the Germans, Adams maintained, enjoyed from the beginnings the benefits of democratic government.

Unfortunately, these benefits did not persist into modern times. Adams developed the thesis that the changes perpetrated by Edward the Confessor brought about the ruin of the legal institutions of the Anglo-Saxons.[42] Because Edward's sympathies were with the Normans, he introduced from the Continent the idea that the rights of the court originally belonged to the crown and could therefore be transferred to private hands. The old democratic ideas of justice were undermined and feudalism was established. For Adams this was a disaster. Today Adams's interpretation seems too much an uncritical acceptance of German historical scholarship, but if his general framework is questionable his meticulous examination of the ancient sources is still valid.

By any standards other than his own, Adams's career as a professor at Harvard was brilliantly successful. The training of students such as Henry Osborne Taylor and Henry Cabot Lodge would in itself entitle him to high academic recognition. He was popular and effective with his undergraduate students. It was not his teaching that brought about his resignation but a disagreement with the publishers of the *North American Review*.[43] Adams, though long associated with the liberal Republicans, felt he could not support Hayes in the election of 1876. Giving his support to Tilden, he sought by means of an editorial in the *North American Review* to influence the readership of the journal to do likewise. His publishers disapproved. They allowed him to print the editorial, but they required disavowal of their support. Adams resigned his editorship as a result. He completed the term of his professorship, but when the opportunity came to edit the papers of Albert Gallatin, Adams used it as an excuse to resign and concentrate on scholarship.[44] Never one to do things by halves, he removed himself from the temptations of Cambridge and took up residence once more in Washington.

V   *Adams at the Verge of Fame*

At the age of thirty-eight Henry Adams had written nothing on which his later fame would depend. If his career had terminated at this point, he would have been known as a brilliant but minor writer who had never touched on subjects of large dimension. Yet he had done a great deal upon which his later career would depend. Perhaps most important, he had acquired the habit of writing, a habit which, he later observed, always leads to a search for something about which to write. He had acquired flexibility of style, and he was already using the irony for which he would become famous. For subject matter he had assimilated the quality of the Adams heritage and had placed its idealism against the background of American history and that of practical nineteenth-century politics. He had examined the intellectual ferment of Victorian England, and he had given the most intense study to European and American history. His preparations for writing history could hardly have been improved.

Because Adams has been so often called a "scientific" historian, it is important at this point to consider his attitude toward determinism in history. He was always interested in science, and he professed himself a follower of Comte, who sought to establish a pattern of determinism in human history.[45] But at this stage of his career, Adams could never have written history from the standpoint of scientific determinism. He was always making moral judgments: he called Captain John Smith mendacious, Jay Gould venal, and Edward the Confessor unjust. As Sir Isaiah Berlin has remarked in his essay "Historical Inevitability," the rendering of such judgments implies freedom of choice and an acceptance of the historian's need for moral responsibility. Avoidance of this function of the historian would have demonstrated a "wish to escape from an untidy, cruel, and above all seemingly purposeless world."[46] Of all Adams's equipment as he moved forward into his productive career, none was more important than the attribute of courage. However much he longed for the comfort of a fixed pattern in history, he could never make it more than a tendency. When Adams perceived the structure of things, it was always from the perspective of an Olympian who could compare, evaluate, and pass final judgment.

CHAPTER 3

Adams the Biographer

THE papers of Albert Gallatin, Secretary of the Treasury under Jefferson, had been lying unused for thirty years when his son Albert Rolaz Gallatin offered them to Henry Adams for editing.[1] The offer came at an opportune time, for Adams was smarting under the loss of his hopes for political reform and his resignation from the editorship of the *North American Review*. Personal considerations aside, the project interested Adams because Gallatin had been so closely associated with his grandfather John Quicy Adams. Both had suffered because of the Embargo, both took part in the negotiations at Ghent which ended the War of 1812, and both had worked against slavery in the agitation that preceded the Civil War. John Quincy Adams many times expressed his respect for Gallatin. Henry Adams's interest in his papers was, once again, an expression of the strongly personal approach which he always took to history.

His removal to Washington freed him from the frenetic activity his heavy teaching load at Harvard required, but it also put him near important collections of papers he needed to consult. He was not only given access to the archives of the State Department,[2] but he was also accorded all the amenities of the new building that would make his research pleasant. Adams spared no effort to obtain access to primary materials. Following the example of German historians whom he admired, he collected copies of thousands of pages of letters and other primary documents. This patient and careful research was, and still remains, one of his most valuable contributions. But it cost him greatly in time: even though he was wealthy enough to be relieved of most of the drudgery of ordinary life and though he was a prodigious worker, he did not publish his *Gallatin* until the summer of 1879, more than two years after he had been given access to the Gallatin papers.

I *The Problem of Interpretation*

Many of those who have read Adams's biography of Gallatin have felt that its author contributed only enough cement of narrative to paste together a collection of letters.[3] It is true that Adams allowed his primary sources to have an unusual proportion of his space, but he did not shirk the problem of interpretation. Basically, he was seeking to account for the development of a man who had acquired the ability to shape the destiny of a nation by the exertion of political power. To do so, he applied a thesis he might well have taken from his Adams forebears: he interpreted Gallatin as developing from a youth of feeling to a man of reason. The thesis has a certain obviousness about it, but it fitted conveniently into the pattern of ideas of nineteenth-century historiography. It allowed Adams to show the unfolding of what was latent in his subject. Gallatin grew up in an age dominated by Rousseau and the cult of feeling, and as a young man he seemed to be given over to those ideas.[4] But this was only the surface, for the deepest element in his native Geneva was Calvinism. Adams's narrative, then, described the gradual peeling away of the layers of Rousseauism acquired in Gallatin's youth to reveal the rationalism which was at the center of his nature. Because the intellectual climate of Geneva had so much affinity with that of Massachusetts in his grandfather's day, Adams could feel entire sympathy with this process of discovery.

II *The Young Gallatin*

True to the search for origins he had learned from the German historians, Adams began his *Life of Albert Gallatin* with an account of his subject's ancestry.[5] He conceded that the Gallatin family's belief that their most famous ancestor was a Roman general could not be proved. But the records going back to 1258 were enough to establish the aristocratic quality of the family. By 1535, when Geneva was established as a city, the Gallatins were among its most prominent families. And for the period of Gallatin's youth, Adams could quote from the correspondence between Madame Gallatin-Vaudenet and Voltaire to show that the family included persons of the highest intellectual capabilities. For Adams and his nineteenth-century audience these credentials would have gone far to establish the worth of young Gallatin.

But Gallatin was emotional and impractical and refused to settle down in his native city to the advantages won for him by his family. Instead, he emigrated to America in 1783. Adams says of him at this stage:

Instead of embracing his opportunities, he repelled them. Like many other brilliant men, he would not, and never did, learn to overcome some youthful prejudices: he disliked great cities and the strife of crowded social life; he never could quite bring himself to believe in their advantages and the necessity of modern society to agglomerate in masses and either to solve the difficulties inherent in close organization or to perish under them. He preferred a wilderness in youth, and, as will be seen, continued in theory to prefer it in his age. It was the instinct of his time and his associations; the atmosphere of Rousseau and Jefferson; pure theory, combined with shy pride.[6]

This romantic side of his nature was given free rein as he wandered about America. During a period of land speculation in western Pennsylvania, he acquired his permanent residence, "Friendship Hill." This was a farm on the Monongahela River, a spot well suited to satisfy the craving for natural beauty of a romantic brought up in Switzerland. Yet the country offered little opportunity for a man of his training. And its unsuitability as a dwelling place at the time was pathetically demonstrated when Gallatin's young wife died there within a few months of their marriage, far from medical assistance.

Adams cannot resist editorializing about Gallatin's choices of his center of operations: "Had Gallatin gone at once to New York or Philadelphia and devoted himself to the law, for which he was admirably fitted by nature, had he invested his little patrimony in a city house, in public securities, in almost any property near at hand and easily convertible, there is every reason to suppose that he would have been, financially and politically, in a better position than was the case in fact."[7] But if Gallatin had been such a clear-sighted rationalist, he might never have entered political life. Raymond Walters stresses his concern for the rights of his western Pennsylvania neighbors, which he felt "almost by instinct."[8] In his first forays into Pennsylvania politics, he showed himself much more emotionally involved than the rank and file. Especially in the Pennsylvania state constitutional convention of 1789–1790, he expressed himself in favor of more democratic provisions than were eventually enacted into law. Only gradually did he move toward the compromises that the rationalist would regard as necessary in politics.

Elected to the Pennsylvania legislature in 1789, Gallatin soon found himself caught between his constituents on the one hand and the federal government on the other. He took the part of moderation in the struggle and succeeded in bringing many of the dissidents to his point of view. Even though he opposed the views of many of his constituents, he was elected to the House of Representatives. So impressive was this accomplishment that Adams explains:

Undoubtedly his mind was one of rare power, perhaps for this especial purpose the most apt that America has ever seen; a mind for which no principle was too broad and no detail too delicate; but it was essentially a scientific and not a political mind. Mr. Gallatin always tended to think with an entire disregard of the emotions; he could only with an effort refrain from balancing the opposing sides of a political question.[9]

Both in the Pennsylvania legislature and in Congress, Gallatin was able to use this inclination to great advantage in his work on finance. Unlike Hamilton and the Federalists, who wanted a sufficient army and navy and who did not object to a national debt, Gallatin and the Republicans stoutly resisted expenditures for an army and a navy, and sought to reduce the national debt.

As much as Adams admires Gallatin, he cannot subscribe entirely to this philsophical position. Gallatin and Jefferson were thinking of the life of unimpassioned reason, like that of the Houyhnhnms in the fourth book of *Gulliver's Travels*. Military equipment by its very presence would encourage men to give expression to the passions, and worse, it would encourage the congregation of men in cities in order to generate the capital required to purchase and employ arms. Ultimately, Gallatin and Jefferson had in mind an emphasis on a type of human personality, a fact which Adams sees and against which he objects: "Mr. Gallatin habitually made too little allowance for the force and complexity of human passions and instincts. Self-contained and self-reliant himself, and, like most close reasoners, distrustful of everything that had a mere feeling for its justification, he held government down to an exact observation of rules that made no allowance for national pride."[10] This reaction to the Rousseauism of his youth was not entirely good, Adams feels. Government, he believes, "has to deal with beings ruled not only by reason but by feeling, and its success depends on the degree to which it can satisfy or at least compromise between the double standard of criticism."[11] Adams undoubtedly was right in his analysis of the weakness of absolute rationalism in government, but the voters of 1800 had swept Jefferson and his theories into power. By that date Gallatin had developed to the point that he was as capable as anyone in the new administration of putting into effect the Republican ideas.

III   Gallatin as Secretary of the Treasury

To begin his chapter on Gallatin's tenure as Secretary of the Treasury, Adams writes wittily and sententiously, "In governments as in households, he who holds the purse holds the power."[12] He was never more serious. Adams was not one to admire mediocrity, but he did admire those who had the force to exercise power for the benefit of the people. The experience of John Adams and John Quincy Adams had taught him that power might or it might not be an accompaniment of the highest office. Sometimes a lesser office might be the real center of an administration. Even under George Washington, Alexander Hamilton had made the Treasury a department of primary importance. In a very different way Gallatin used the same office to exercise power.

Although Adams often disagreed with Republican practice in the government, his chapter on "The Treasury" paints a sympathetic picture of Gallatin.[13] Under Jefferson he had an especially great responsibility, for the third President had, so Adams thought, an inclination to be excessively theoretical. Jefferson understood that government under the Constitution must be made to serve the interests of a larger proportion of the people than it had under the Federalists. He saw that Hamilton's distrust of the people was a great impediment to the development of a strong allegiance to the new government in a large proportion of the population. The various measures which he supported—among them states' rights, the limitation of military force, and the reduction of the national debt—were well calculated to bring about the effects he desired. But theoretical abstractions could never by themselves carry on the day-to-day affairs of the government. Gallatin supplied the hard core of practical realism that enabled the ideas of Jefferson to be brought into effective use.

When Gallatin acceded to the Treasury in 1801, he set to work to implement the extinguishment of the national debt.[14] His priority did not indicate mere anti-Federalism, though it went exactly counter to Hamilton's "a national debt is a national blessing." Instead, like other Republicans, he looked on the debt as a source of possible manipulation and corruption. The rock on which he based all his fiscal planning was the rapid removal of the debt, which he expected to accomplish by 1817. Gallatin found that the sum of $7,300,000 per year was required to service the debt, and he planned his entire budget around this figure.

With so large a sum appropriated for the debt out of a total expected revenue of slightly less than $10 million, Gallatin was forced to use his discretionary powers to limit expenditures in other fields. Good Republican that he was, he proposed to spend only about a million and a half on both army and navy. Adams balks at Gallatin's penuriousness, which would have left the country exposed to foreign conquest. But for Gallatin the dangers of a large military establishment were greater than those of possible conquest by a foreign power remote from American shores. Unfortunately, he was never able to keep military appropriations as low as his projected figures when he first took office. He did repay the debt at the rate he suggested, but he had to find other revenue to meet the expenses of the military, which were greatly increased because of the war with the Barbary pirates. But because he kept the Treasury in good financial condition for his main purpose of the extinguishment of the debt, he did not find the increases burdensome.

Gallatin's mastery of finance enabled him to weather with relative equanimity the unexpected crisis in 1803 of the Louisiana Purchase.[15] As Jefferson himself felt, the purchase of Louisiana made a mockery of the Constitution. But such a windfall could not be ignored even by the scrupulous Jefferson—he knew that the purchase must be consummated before Napoleon had time to change his mind. Because Gallatin did not share Jefferson's doubts about the legality of the purchase, he did not hesitate to apply to his friend Alexander Baring, the English banker, for funds. Fortunately, the credit of the country was good. Gallatin had only to make small adjustments of his budget for the increased sums required for the service of the debt and for the necessary taxes. Though Jefferson's worries about the loose construction of the Constitution remained, the practical Gallatin kept his attention on the less rarefied circumstances of his office.

So successful was Gallatin in his management of the Treasury that by 1806 he had accumulated a large surplus and had begun to think of internal improvements on which the money might be spent. A national university, turnpikes, and canals were among the projects he contemplated. But all his plans were brought to naught by the financial difficulties of the Treasury during the Embargo.[16] Gallatin's carefully worked out surplus became a deficit, and improvements had to be indefinitely postponed. For Adams this defeat for Gallatin takes on the character of tragedy.

Adams tends to blame Jefferson for the Embargo. As President Jefferson allowed his abhorrence of military force to blind him to the realities of the condition of Europe during the Napoleonic wars. Perhaps most pathetic was Jefferson's gunboat scheme. Instead of building large vessels of war that might be useful in case of conflict with France or England, he decided upon a fleet of two hundred little gunboats for coastal defense. Gallatin and others remonstrated against this plan, but Jefferson would take no advice. As Gallatin expected, the gunboats were both ineffective and expensive. Worse, they gave Jefferson nothing with which to negotiate with France and England, both of which were threatening American commerce. Eventually matters came to a crisis when the British ship *Leopard* attacked the American ship *Chesapeake* and forced her to strike her colors. In those days of hair-trigger response to national insult, this incident called for a declaration of war. But Jefferson, unprepared for war and anxious for peace, demurred. Months after the *Chesapeake-Leopard* affair, he put into effect a measure short of war, the Embargo.

At this stage of his narrative, Adams makes the contrast between Jefferson and Gallatin sharpest. On the one hand, the theory-ridden Jefferson could hardly bring himself to exercise some of the most important powers of his office. Adams's comment seems rather bitter: "There was but one respectable policy,—war, immediate and irrespective of cost or risk; but of war all parties stood in dread, and as between England and France it was difficult to choose an opponent."[17] Obviously Adams is thinking less of the cost of war than he is of the need for the Executive to use power. Especially when Jefferson had a Secretary of the Treasury who was adept at the use of the resources of his office, the President himself seemed weaker by contrast.

Perhaps some of Adams's tone can be attributed to sectionalism. The Embargo was sectional and political in its inception because it was imposed by an agrarian, Republican group in the government against a commercial, Federalist section. The stopping of New England ships meant that most of the cost of the Embargo was borne by the Northeast. Although the section eventually profited by being forced away from commerce into manufacturing, the memories of Jefferson's hurt lingered long, as Sarah Orne Jewett reflected so often in her sketches of the seacoast villages of Maine. Adams, too, seems to have felt the injustice of Jefferson's policy.

Adams is constantly at pains to point up the dictatorial control necessary for the implementation of the Embargo. Gallatin had predicted that such would be the case, but once the law was enacted he loyally tried to enforce it. Adams feels that Gallatin was almost entirely the victim of his own highmindedness and the circumstances around him. But later commentators have been somewhat less kind. They stress the shortsightedness of his dependence on an impost and his failure to keep alternative measures of taxation in readiness. So the failure of the Embargo was, at least in some measure, Gallatin's failure as well as Jefferson's.

Because Adams so clearly recognizes the place of power in politics, he cannot help registering discontent with the foreign policy of the years preceding the War of 1812. The ineffectualness of the Embargo was followed by a weakly vacillating policy in the Madison administration.[18] As Adams explains, the theory of Republicanism decentralized the government so much that it could not function effectively as a unit in negotiations with other governments. In all the manifestations of power by which nations indicated their standing—its army, its navy, its public buildings, even the style of its executive—the United States was weak. After the Embargo, the Treasury, which under Gallatin had shown promise of becoming a source of power, fell into grave ineffectuality.

Exasperated by these conditions, Adams breaks into his narrative to comment that the United States should have ordered an immediate attack on Napoleon in 1809. This attack would have been successful, he remarks, and it would also have frightened the English as well.[19] Adams's interpretation at this point tells more about his own ideas than it does about international affairs in 1809. Obviously no one could have been sure of the outcome of an attack on Napoleon. For a nation of about 7 million to attack one of 28 million would require some temerity, especially as the latter had a military genius as head of state. But Adams has no need to plan responsibly:

he is theorizing long after the fact. He suggests that if there had been interest enough in power in the central administration in Washington, then the government would have supported such an attack with military and financial support sufficient to cause Napoleon to respect its position. The need for effectiveness would cause a sufficient response, provided the means were at hand. Perhaps the most difficult part of Adams's argument for a later generation to swallow is his faith in military power. Like many of his generation, he minimizes the cost of the military operations of 1861–1865 because he was impressed with their outcome.

Adams depicts with sympathy the struggles of Gallatin in the Treasury during the Madison administration, but he admits that Gallatin's effectiveness was ended by 1811.[20] Defeated in his request for rechartering the Bank of the United States, he found himself embarrassed to borrow funds for the conduct of the war. He continued to rely heavily on import duties, even though the war obviously meant their reduction. And even though the taxes Gallatin proposed were insufficient, he could not persuade Congress to enact even those requests. Gallatin's reasons for leaving the Treasury are not known, but Adams speculates that it was his ineffectiveness in securing revenue that caused him to leave on a diplomatic mission to Russia without having resigned as Secretary.[21]

IV *Diplomat and Scholar*

Gallatin's appointment to the peace commission at the end of the War of 1812 gave him one of his greatest personal successes. His mission did not begin auspiciously; he spent nearly three months in St. Petersburg in what would have been fruitless waiting except for his opportunity to become closely acquainted with John Quincy Adams. More months of negotiations ensued in England while the British made up their minds to negotiate. Finally, the commissioners assembled at Ghent in August 1814. The Americans had little with which to work against the world's greatest power except their skill in diplomacy. Of the three American commissioners Adams gives most credit to Gallatin; he was the one who kept peace between the combative John Quincy Adams and Henry Clay.[22] The negotiations dragged on for months, but the British reluctance to expend more on war prevailed, and the treaty was signed on Christmas Day 1814. The commercial negotiations that followed kept Gallatin in England for another six months: he finally reached home in July 1815.

Though he was immediately appointed Ambassador to France,[23] he delayed a year in taking up his duties. He spent seven years in this office, among the most pleasant in his life. He was the most skillful diplomat in the service, Adams declares, and his abilities were held in high esteem by the government. But he was necessarily preoccupied with details of a commercial nature, and he felt that this mission had not allowed him to function at his greatest usefulness. Yet, after he returned home in 1823, it was this skill that led to his next appointment. President John Quincy Adams sent him in 1826 to negotiate with Great Britain concerning problems of commerce and the boundaries of Maine and Oregon.[24] Gallatin employed his usual tact and patience to good effect, and he brought his diplomatic career to a close with the signing of a convention in July 1827.

Adams treats the last nineteen years of Gallatin's life briefly, as perhaps fitted their place in the sum total of this active man's life. He wrote "Considerations on the Currency and Banking System of the United States" in 1830, a worthy consideration of the early financial history of the country;[25] although it was not written as a political document, it was circulated by the Bank of the United States, then under attack by the Jacksonians. Gallatin's position did not prevail, but he continued his interest in finance by himself becoming associated with a private bank, a position which he held for a number of years.

Another of Gallatin's interests leads Adams to give him the title of "father of American ethnology."[26] He collected great numbers of examples of Indian vocabulary, and he spent immense effort in the classification of Indian languages. He described the linguistic groups of the North American Indians, and he made the first ethnographical map of merit of North America.

If Adams admires Gallatin for his realism, scholarship, and diplomacy, he must have been even more impressed by one of the final gestures of his life: his "Speech on the Annexation of Texas."[27] Gallatin spoke at a popular meeting in New York on the negative side of the proposition, stressing the idea that to annex Texas would mean war. He emphasized that he would be against disturbing slavery wherever it existed, but that he would be against its extension.

This was the same position for which John Quincy Adams was fighting in Congress. Both men continued the fight, each in his way, almost to the moment of death, which came for Gallatin only about a year after that of his friend.

V *Evaluation*

Adams himself admirably summed up his estimate of Gallatin in a letter of October 6, 1879, to Henry Cabot Lodge:

To my mind the moral of his life lies a little deeper than party politics and I have tried here and there rather to suggest than to assert it. The inevitable isolation and disillusionment of a really strong mind—one that combines force with elevation—is to me the romance and tragedy of statesmanship. The politician who goes to his grave without suspecting his own limitations, is not a picturesque figure; he is only an animal. That old beggar who was an Emperor somewhere, and on his death-bed asked his weeping friends: "Have I not acted my part well?"; that man was picturesque. Gallatin was greater, because he could and did refuse power when he found out what vanity it was, and yet became neither a cynic nor a transcendental philosopher.[28]

Adams's biography, then, is not a tragedy, as some scholars have maintained. It is an account of the transformation of an emotional youth into a man of reason who used his own freedom of choice to make whatever adjustments to circumstance were required. Nothing could speak better for him than his dignity in old age, when he met his duty as he saw it and continued a full functioning human being to the very end.

CHAPTER 4

John Randolph

TRYING to isolate the qualities that New England had imparted to his nature, Henry Adams devised in the *Education* a Law of Resistance, a principle which he thought explained many of his choices.[1] Though he obviously intended some irony, in one respect he did not: his resistance to things and persons Southern persisted all his life. The habit had been established in his family long before he was born. The estrangement of John Adams and Thomas Jefferson had lasted many years before their final reconciliation in extreme old age. John Quincy Adams had shown strong antipathy for the Virginian John Randolph over a very long period. But the greatest problem for all the Adamses was that of slavery. When Henry made his first trip to Washington at the age of twelve, he was appalled at the slovenliness which allowed cows and pigs and Negro babies to mingle in such a way as to suggest that they might all occupy the same cabin.[2] Though the Maryland blood of his grandmother Adams made him somewhat tolerant of the ease of the Southerner, his paternal inheritance marked slavery as the sum of all wickedness. As he grew older his antipathy to the South did not lessen. At Harvard he became well acquainted with Roony Lee, the son of Robert E. Lee, of whom he wrote, "Strictly, the Southerner had no mind; he had temperament."[3] Adams regarded him as a relic of the stone age, unfit for modern life. The partisanship of the Civil War tended, quite naturally, to confirm Adams's antipathy for Southerners.

In the *Life of Gallatin* Adams did not conceal his sympathy for the Pennsylvania branch of the Republican party, which was not always in accord with its Southern members. John Randolph of Virginia was one especially singled out for unfavorable attention. Despite Adams's obvious lack of sympathy for Randolph, John T. Morse, Jr., the editor of the "American Statesmen" series, asked Adams to

prepare the volume on Randolph.[4] At the time Adams was occupied
with his projected history of the Jefferson and Madison administrations. He hesitated to take on the assignment, but then agreed.
Although Adams always deprecated the book and Morse came to
question his own judgment in assigning it to someone so hostile,
neither had any reason for regret. *John Randolph* contains some of
Adams's most colorful writing: its witty ironies anticipate by nearly
half a century the style of biography practiced by Lytton Strachey.

I *Virginia Boyhood*

As his narrative stance Adams chooses an Olympian pose which
separates him from inconvenient sympathy for his subject. He
frankly admits that he is a New England man looking with some
disbelief at this Virginian. In contrast to the stern discipline of the
New England winter with its strictness of schooling and with par-
ents and grandparents committed to the life of reason, Adams thinks
that life in the South was much easier: "Many a Virginian lad, especially on such a remote plantation as Bizarre, lived in a boy's
paradise of indulgence, fished and shot, rode like a young monkey,
and had his memory crammed with the genealogy of every well-
bred horse in the State, grew up among dogs and Negroes, master
equally of both, and knew all about the prices of wheat, tobacco, and
slaves."[5] Adams, who would later confess to liking the carefree life
out of doors at Quincy in the summer, nevertheless grows uneasy at
the thought of so much self-indulgence: "The climate was genial, the
soil generous, the life easy, the temptations strong."[6] Neither did
Virginia offer Randolph the kind of reading that would develop his
intellect; far too many of the books he knew appealed to his imagination rather than his reason—the Arabian Nights, Shakespeare,
Homer, *Don Quixote, Tom Jones.* Adams believes that "the kind of
literary diet on which the boy thus fed was not the healthiest or best
for a nature like his."[7] But in his inclinations he was only following
what those around him also did: "He was a true Virginian, a son of
the soil and the time."[8]

Early in his career John Randolph's character became fixed, so
Adams believes, "as pure a Virginian Quixote as ever an American
Cervantes could have conceived."[9] His peculiar aberration Adams
describes: "His mind was always controlled by his feelings; its an-
tipathies were stronger than its sympathy; it was restless and uneasy, prone to contradiction and attached to paradox."[10] All that a

person of this inclination needed was to find himself a hobbyhorse, and unfortunately for Randolph one was near at hand. He had merely to follow the course of the feeling in Virginia against the centralizing tendencies in the national government and he would have a fixed center for his entire life.

Randolph's antipathy to Federalism may have received its greatest impetus from his memories of his brother's treatment at John Adams's inaugural as Vice-President.[11] Approaching too closely to the official carriage, the boy was driven back by the coachman's whip. John Randolph carried with him for forty years the memory of this little scene. Henry Adams believes that Randolph did not resent the coachman's act in itself; it was the low social standing of the Vice-President that made the deed rankle. But, as even Adams admits, it was not complete irrationality that started Randolph toward anti-Federalism. The Republican party, of which he became a member, had underlying its theory of government "the historical fact that political power had, in all experience, tended to grow at the expense of human liberty."[12] And, as Adams rather grudgingly concedes, "so far as his wayward life had a meaning or a moral purpose, it lay in his strenuous effort to bar the path of that spirit of despotism which in every other age and land had perverted government into a curse and a scourge."[13]

II *Early Career*

John Randolph began his career as a States' Rights man, one committed to the Jeffersonian principle that the federal government should be turned into a machine with strictly limited powers. He carried his ideas against the opposition of Patrick Henry so successfully that Adams terms his abilities "genius."[14] He was elected to the House of Representatives in 1799, when he was only twenty-six years old. And only two years later he was chosen chairman of the Ways and Means Committee.[15] For him and for his Republican colleagues the world seemed to be beginning anew. Randolph and his friends wished to write the principles of the Republican victory of 1800 into law, but they were unable to secure legislation to curb any of the powers of the federal government. Adams blames both Randolph and Jefferson, who had exaggerated the menace of the Federalists. Calling John Adams a monarchist, they sent him away, but they failed to recognize that Jefferson himself appeared somewhat in the same guise as he was forced to exercise the powers of his office. Ironically, in carrying out the Louisiana Purchase, Jefferson was forced to use powers far beyond those considered acceptable by States' Rights men. Randolph, Adams points out, was totally inconsistent on this point: "He who had raged with the violence of a wild animal against the constitutional theories of Washington and John Adams did not whisper a remonstrance against this new assumption of power, which, according to Mr. Jefferson, made blank paper of the Constitution."[16] And in governing the new territory, he permitted Jefferson to exercise powers as despotic as those of the King of Spain.

Adams gives heavy emphasis to Randolph's concern with the judiciary,[17] which was a major problem for the entire Republican party. John Adams had thwarted their desire for weakening the power of the judges by appointing John Marshall Chief Justice of the Supreme Court. But even so strong a personality as he would not have been able to make the judiciary impregnable if it were not for the provision in the Constitution which limited the causes for which judges could be removed to those of actual wrongdoing. Unlike the English system, which permitted removal by Parliament by simple address, the American was unresponsive to changes in political opinion. Judges could override the wishes of the people themselves and could thereby augment the power of the central government. This condition threatened the doctrine which Randolph regarded as most important of all—that of states' rights. Yet the actions of the Republicans on their accession to power were comparatively mild. In 1802 Randolph introduced a motion to inquire into the condition of the judiciary, and he helped to secure the repeal of the Judiciary Act of 1800 by which the Federalists had increased the number of judges. Up to this point, Adams feels, Randolph acted in a manner which enhanced his reputation.

But Randolph's emotions would not let him be satisfied, and the part he played in the removal of Judge Pickering helped to excite Federalist suspicions that he might be seeking to establish precedent for removal without cause.[18] Judge Pickering had become mentally incompetent and was therefore an easy target, but his case was quickly followed by a much more controversial one—that of Justice Chase of the Supreme Court.[19] Although Jefferson himself expressed privately his wish for the removal of the obnoxious Justice, he allowed others to take the public exposure. Randolph willingly accepted the role of manager of the proceedings against Chase for the House of Representatives. Because Randolph wanted to be sure of impeaching Chase, he chose to frame some of the articles of impeachment on grounds of criminality and judicial error. In so doing, Randolph played into the hands of the Federalists, who had assembled the best legal talent in the country for the defense of Justice Chase. The attorneys available to the House were by no means the equal of those for the defense. Randolph's own speeches, as reported by such hostile witnesses as John Quincy Adams, were prolix, rambling, and charged with excessive emotionality. Other scholars have disputed Adams's interpretation, citing his own capacity for virulence, but though this charge has been disputed,[20] Henry Adams accepted the word of his grandfather. Probably partisan politics had a great deal to do with the failure to obtain the necessary two-thirds for conviction, but it was a severe blow for Randolph.

Henry Adams looks upon the failure as a personal one: "On no other occasion in Randolph's life was he compelled to follow a long and consecutive train of thought within the bounds of logical method, and his arguments at this trial are therefore the only exact test of his reasoning powers. His failure was decided."[21] The weakness of excessive emotionality delivered him over to his enemies completely: the precedent established at this trial made impregnable the position of Chief Justice John Marshall, who was establishing the Supreme Court as the body for deciding questions of the interpretation of the Constitution. And with this trial, the influence of Randolph over his fellow Republicans came to an end. From this point on, Adams finds that Randolph's effectiveness steadily diminished.

III *Randolph in Opposition*

Adams dates confidently the time at which Randolph began his career of opposition: March 5, 1806.[22] The occasion was a debate in Congress about the attacks on American trade by the British. Randolph, as was consistent with his Republican outlook, took a stand against the military. But to his call for negotiation with the British, he added an attack on Jefferson and Gallatin. About a month later, he declared himself no longer a Republican; denominating himself a member of a third party, he contemptuously adopted for it the label *tertium quid,* or "third something." His real bias, so Adams feels, was against the Secretary of State, James Madison. So violent was his antipathy to Madison that he made several breaches of personal confidence in his attempt to undermine Madison's negotiations with France for the purchase of Florida. All of this activity, Adams feels, was completely negative: "Randolph was left a political wreck; the true Virginian school of politics was forever ruined; Macon was soon driven from the speakership; and Nicholson forced on to the bench; Gallatin was paralyzed; Mr. Jefferson, Mr. Madison, and ultimately Mr. Monroe were thrown into the hands of the northern democrats, whose loose political morality henceforward found no check; the spirit of intrigue was stimulated, and the most honest and earnest convictions of the republican party were discredited."[23] Certainly Adams is paying Randolph's irrationality the highest possible compliment; he would unquestionably have been the most powerful man in government could he have singlehandedly done so much. Then Adams adds, "The story of Randolph's famous quarrel with his party has now been told in a spirit as friendly to him as his friends can require or expect,—has been told, so far as possible in his own words, without prejudice or passion, and shall be left to be judged on its merits."[24] Certainly it would seem that Adams is here wittily undercutting himself as narrator: he knows as well as anyone the Adams quarrel with Randolph. And he also knows the human tendency to choose a worthy adversary. John Quincy Adams chose to do battle with Randolph because to vanquish him would confer honor.

Adams's picture of Randolph emphasizes more and more his ineffectiveness in politics because of his own bad motives. Adams remarks, "Randolph's temper was now ugly beyond what was to be expected from a man whose objects were only to serve the public and to secure honest government. His hatred of the northern democrats broke out in ways which showed a wish to rule or ruin."[25] His opposition to a bill to prohibit the slave trade reflected such a spirit and more: "Besides attempting thus to stir up trouble between the South and North, he made a desperate effort to put the Senate and House at odds, and showed a spirit of pure venom that went far to sink his character as an honest man."[26] When the Republicans wished to nominate Madison as Jefferson's successor, Randolph sought to stir up feeling against Madison. Adams comments: "Not patriotism, but revenge, inspired Randolph's passion; the impulse to strike down those whom he chose to hate."[27] During this campaign, which Madison won handily, Randolph drank excessively, a habit in which he indulged off and on for the remainder of his life. Again Adams editorializes: "Probably in consequence of this license his mind showed signs of breaking down. He was at times distinctly irrational, though never quite incapable of self-control."[28] During the campaign of 1813 the Richmond *Enquirer* called him "a nuisance and a curse." His opposition to the war with England brought about his defeat.

When he was reelected to Congress in 1815, Randolph readied a new weapon with which to fight for states' rights. He joined forces with the slave power, though in his early career he had opposed it. With it he was a formidable ally, because his kind of oratory would be understood and appreciated in the South. Adams declares, "Neither his oratory nor his wit would have been tolerated in a northern State. To the cold-blooded New Englander who did not love extravagance or eccentricity, and had no fancy for plantation manners, Randolph was an obnoxious being."[29] But in his own district he knew how to use flattery, courtesy, and terror to gain his ends. At this time in his career, his emotions had been perverted into instruments to be used by his reason: "His insulting language and manner came not from the heart, but from the head: they were part of his system, a method of controlling society as he controlled his negroes."[30] Yet only a few pages later Adams observes in a somewhat contradictory statement: "The better part of his nature made a spasmodic struggle against the passions and appetites that degraded it. Half his rudeness and savagery was due to pride which would allow no one to see the full extent of his weakness."[31]

Adams concedes that Randolph's opposition to the Presidency of John Quincy Adams had a solid foundation: because Randolph had remained a States' Rights man, John Quincy Adams's desire to use federal revenues for internal improvements—the "American System"—placed him in the opposite camp. Randolph used biting invective as his chief weapon for fighting Adams. He claimed to have been "defeated, horse, foot, and dragoons,—cut up and clean broke down by the coalition of Blifil and Black George—by the combination, unheard of till then, of the Puritan with the blackleg."[32] John Quincy Adams himself managed to stay apart from Randolph's attacks, but Clay was eventually drawn into a duel with him in which, however, neither was injured. Controversy with the Adams administration, however, suited perfectly Randolph's purpose of consolidating the South as a slave power: the nationalism of John

Quincy Adams as well as his Puritanism gave Randolph the opposition in philosophy he needed to unite the slave states. After he failed to be reelected to the Senate, he was sent by President Jackson on a diplomatic mission to Russia, at the end of which he drew $21,407 from the government—according to Adams, "the most flagrant bit of diplomatic jobbery in the annals of the United States government."[33] Yet despite Jackson's favors, Randolph made speeches in support of South Carolina's position in the nullification controversy. A short time later, he died in Philadelphia while returning to England for his health. Ironically, his last will, which did not emancipate his slaves, was set aside by the court in favor of an earlier one which gave them their freedom.

IV   Evaluation

John Randolph illustrates very well some of the ideas of Edward H. Carr about the psychological problems which must be faced in the writing of history.[34] Carr believes that the reader must observe the mental processes of the historian no less than the historian himself must take into account the minds of his subjects. In *John Randolph* the reader encounters an Adams more passionate than in any other of his writings. He takes up the defense of John Adams and John Quincy Adams with a vigor he was too polite to show in the *Gallatin* or the *History* or even in the *Education.* Frequently he is so partisan that he criticizes Randolph for a polemical stand that would clearly seem within the limits of congressional oratory. Some of his strictures against Randolph's personal honesty and his intellectual consistency seem exaggerated. Adams appears to be projecting onto Randolph a part of his own personality which he fears and seeks to repress or to control. At Harvard Adams was the rebel, both as student and professor, but he was the disciplined scholar in writing *Gallatin.* He saw in Randolph the perennial little boy, always moving into opposition to test the convictions and character of his elders. Adams, too, would have liked the pose, but he was well aware that it had a ludicrous side. By showing it in Randolph, he must have found purgation of his own desire.

Certainly his portrait of Randolph differs greatly from that of some of those who have followed him. The Virginians, as Adams himself pointed out, have always managed to take Randolph seriously. Russell Kirk does even more: he gives Randolph a high place among conservative thinkers in America. Randolph rejected the leveling ideas of the Declaration of Independence and substituted in their stead aristocratic principles. According to Kirk, for him, "the real and ineradicable sources of political power are vigor of mind and body, possession of property. Equality and fraternity, far from being natural rights, are artificial conventions, to be extended or contracted as the requirements of a particular society dictate. As for liberty, individual and natural freedom, although it was not an abstract right of man, it was a natural objective."[35] Certainly Adams never took Randolph this seriously. Perhaps the truth about this strange Virginian may lie in some composite picture that takes into account both the seriousness of Kirk's interpretation and the quixotic attitude of Adams.

CHAPTER 5

Democracy

WHEN the novel *Democracy* was published anonymously in 1880, it immediately attracted attention because it was so obviously a *roman à clef*, full of an insider's knowledge of the political scene in Washington. Curiosity about the author's identity stirred up interest in the book, which soon went through several printings. For a time Marian Adams was suspected of being its author; then attention shifted to John Hay; and even Henry Adams himself came in for some attention. But the secret was so well kept that the book's authorship was not finally confirmed until Henry Holt wrote in 1923 about the circumstances of its publication.[1]

I *The Novel as Satire*

The irony of the title *Democracy* falls upon the American people and their representatives alike: Washington is filled with corruption, but, as Mrs. Lee writes in her note at the very end of the book, the greed of the people themselves is ultimately responsible. Adams the satirist saw very clearly the defects of his own age, but he was helped to do so by the pose of the eighteenth-century man, as he always called himself. The rigid integrity of John Quincy Adams provided a reference point for judging human nature. Although Henry Adams had himself printed enough during the first Grant administration to make the nation want to reform its government, no such reform had taken place. Instead, the Crédit Mobilier exposé of 1872 had revealed that many high officials, including the Vice-President, had been involved in a scheme to get profit from the national government in the building of the Union Pacific Railroad.[2] Then in 1874 the Treasury Department was involved in a scheme to give John D. Sanborn a 50 percent commission for collecting money owed to the government. Grant's Secretary of the Treasury resigned rather than face the censure of Congress for his part in the scheme.

54

In 1875 the Whiskey Ring scandal broke: agents of the government were defrauding it of part of its revenue from the excise tax on whiskey. The President's personal secretary was involved, but Grant resented the investigation. Even the accession of Hayes was not of much help, for men like James G. Blaine were still in the leadership of the Republican party. A country corrupt enough to permit so much wrongdoing in its officials might be too cynical for direct censure, but it might be touched by laughter in the manner of Pope or Swift or Fielding.

Once again Adams relies upon his ability to give his subjects Lilliputian dimensions. All his people are diminutives whose perspectives include little beyond their own selfish interests. Even his best characters show none of the heroic awareness of a Hamlet or an Antony, for they are so locked into the pattern of Washington that they seem to have little freedom of choice. Yet Adams makes clear that if they could increase their awareness they could see that they are bound only by the Lilliputians' threads. In other words, they are not tragic, but comic, figures. If Adams's readers can be brought to laugh at them, then they should understand that they, too, are like these inhabitants of Washington and have an obligation to assert themselves and to change.

II   *Corrupt Politicians*

The irony in Adams's title *Democracy* derives from the contrast of the idealism implicit in the word with the realities of the practice of government in Washington. For Adams, the very type of the corrupt official is James G. Blaine, the Senator from Maine, who is transformed in *Democracy* into Silas P. Ratcliffe, Senator from Illinois. Adams concedes his capability: he knows how to unite the party after the bruising effects of an election and he is able to flatter the new President into the concessions that must be made for the sake of the party.

Yet it is the shortsightedness of party spirit that vitiates his good qualities. In a scene set at Mount Vernon, Adams allows Ratcliffe to expatiate on the character of George Washington: "A respectable, painstaking President, he was treated by the Opposition with an amount of deference that would have made government easy to a baby, but it worried him to death. His official papers are fairly done, and contain good average sense such as a hundred thousand men in the United States would now write."[3] Ratcliffe avers that

Washington had a weakness that would totally incapacitate him for office today: "He stood outside of politics. The thing couldn't be done today. The people don't like that sort of royal airs."[4] And finally he avers, "If Washington were President now, he would have to learn our ways or lose the next election. Only fools and theorists imagine that our society can be handled with gloves or long poles. One must make one's self a part of it. If virtue won't answer our purpose, we must use vice, or our opponents will put us out of office, and this was as true in Washington's day as it is now, and always will be."[5]

A man so far gone in depravity is admirably suited for organizing the party claims to patronage on the eve of the arrival in Washington of the new President. At this point, Adams breaks into his narrative to comment: "The beauty of his work consisted in the skill with which he evaded questions of principle. As he wisely said, the issue now involved was not one of principle but of power. The fate of that noble party to which they all belonged, and which had a record that could never be forgotten, depended on their letting principles alone. Their principle must be the want of principles."[6] This philosophy suits Ratcliffe's purpose of securing control of the new President before he can make his appointments. By means of spies, harassment, and intrigue, the President is badgered into appointing party stalwarts to key positions, the chief of which is the Treasury Department for Silas P. Ratcliffe.

Adams's portrait of the President makes a deeply ironical contrast with the real second and sixth Presidents. "Old Granite" is the product of a democratic electorate which wishes to place in office people like themselves. He originally worked in a quarry, hence his name, and he presumably has the virtues of his occupation—honesty and the capacity for hard work. But he is totally unfit in ability and training to cope with the complexities of the office, especially those thrown in his way by the brilliant and unscrupulous Ratcliffe. Adams's picture of the new President's difficulties is telling:

No maid-of-all-work in a cheap boarding-house was ever more harassed. Everyone conspired against him. His enemies gave him no peace. All Washington was laughing at his blunders, and ribald sheets, published on a Sunday, took delight in printing the new Chief Magistrate's sayings and doings, chronicled with outrageous humor, and placed by malicious hands where the President could not but see them. He was sensitive to ridicule, and it mortified him to the heart to find that remarks and acts, which to him seemed sensible enough, should be capable of such perversion.[7]

After so much frustration it is little wonder that the President surrenders the direction of affairs to Ratcliffe, and even feels relief at having someone take the burden of office from his shoulders. Adams concludes, "Ratcliffe's work was done. The public had, with the help of some clever intrigue, driven its servants into the traces. Even an Indiana stone-cutter could be taught that his personal prejudices must yield to the public service. What mischief the selfishness, the ambition, or the ignorance of these men might do, was another matter. As the affair stood, the President was the victim of his own schemes."[8]

But if Ratcliffe feels complacent about his place in the new administration, he ought to remember a principle that Adams declares inevitable: "Whenever a man reaches the top of the political ladder, his enemies unite to pull him down. His friends become critical and exacting."[9] Sibyl, Madeleine Lee's sister, and Carrington, who wishes to marry Madeleine, join forces against Ratcliffe. Carrington is the executor of the will of Samuel Baker, who had been privy to much political intrigue. Among his papers is material incriminating Ratcliffe. When Carrington can no longer stand the prospect of Madeleine's marrying Ratcliffe, he gives a sealed letter to Sibyl; in the event Madeleine expresses her intention to marry Ratcliffe, Sibyl is to give her the letter. Madeleine declares her intention to marry, Sibyl delivers the letter,[10] and Ratcliffe is exposed as the senator who had accepted a bribe of $100,000 from the Inter-Oceanic Mail Steamship Company for reporting out of committee a bill for a subsidy, which was then passed by Congress. When Madeleine confronts Ratcliffe with this information, he claims never to have seen any money, all of which was given to the party. But Madeleine rejects him, and in his final appearance in the book he is struck in the face by old Baron Jacobi, the worldly-wise Bulgarian minister. Ratcliffe suppresses the impulse to strike back and retires, presumably to return to his political intrigue.

Oddly enough, Adams's villain—or villains, if the President can be counted—emerge better than he probably intended. No doubt Ratcliffe's political philosophy is detestable, as are his manipulation of the patronage and his venality. But the speeches in which he describes his philosophy and admits his guilt have a certain forthrightness which goes far to remove blame from him. He has loyalty to his party. And he seems fortunate in his enemies. Sibyl and Carrington, though in many respects admirable persons, conspire against Ratcliffe in such a way as to transfer some of the reader's sympathy to him. And Baron Jacobi's physical attack on Ratcliffe seems like that of Preston Brooks on Charles Sumner in the Congress. Because Adams shows himself perfectly capable of creating an almost totally unfavorable picture of Jay Gould and James Fisk, it is surprising to find him showing sympathy for Ratcliffe. Perhaps he, too, has that fascination with great evildoers that allows some to put Lucifer so close to God.

III   *The Satiric Norm: Nathan Gore*

Although Nathan Gore plays only a small part in the action of the novel, he is important as a person who is touched by the political process and who emerges with very different ideas from those of Silas Ratcliffe.[11] He has written a *History of Spain in America*, which has made him the dean of American historians and won for him an appointment as Minister at Madrid. But his appointment lapsed some years ago and he is back in Washington seeking to return to Spain. Adams gives him such qualities as selfishness, egotism, and vanity, but he pointedly omits making him venal and corrupt. His only concessions to politics are an ability to eschew satire and the equally important habit of holding his tongue.

Despite his discretion, he is caught in a conversation with Ratcliffe, who asks him, "Do you yourself think democracy the best government, and universal suffrage a success?"[12] His answer seems close to one that Adams might have given in a similar situation. He flatly declares that he believes in democracy. But he does not justify his belief by an abstract analysis of the nature of man. Instead, he says, "I believe in it because it appears to me the inevitable consequence of what has gone before it. Democracy asserts the fact that the masses are now raised to higher intelligence than formerly."[13] In other words, he is presenting a belief in progress which amounts to a belief in the evolution of man from a creature of a lower intelligence to one of a higher. This is complacent nineteenth-century optimism, with which Ratcliffe and most of his listeners would have agreed.

But he is qualifying his position somewhat when he labels democracy an experiment, for this allows him to imply his reservations about what Ratcliffe is doing. Obviously he intends an irony, for democracy will have to be enormously strong to withstand the pressures put upon it by corrupt politicians. His label allows him to insinuate a little sermon: "It is the only direction society can take that is worth its taking; the only conception of its duty large enough to satisfy its instincts; the only result that is worth an effort or a risk. Every other possible step is backward, and I do not care to repeat the past. I am glad to see society grapple with issues in which no one can afford to be neutral."[14] The hint that the present order may tumble into the chaos of the past and that the whole evolutionary process may be lost is too much for either the understanding or the conscience of Ratcliffe, and he is silent.

Mrs. Lee, however, picks up the hint and asks, "Suppose society destroys itself with universal suffrage, corruption, and communism."[15] To this Gore responds by asking that she come with him some evening to the Observatory. There she can see for herself how insignificant our solar system appears among the millions of stars in the universe. She can understand how small would be the loss if one satellite should plunge into its star.[16] At this point Gore seems ready to base a pessimistic interpretation of man's destiny on scientific determinism. But, like Adams himself, he refuses to surrender to the blind forces he sees operating in the universe. Assuming his own freedom to choose his social destiny, he proclaims his faith in democracy and professes his willingness to work to have it prevail.

He concludes by declaring that he has faith: "faith in human nature; faith in science; faith in the survival of the fittest."[17] He implies that these new articles of faith may be no more permanent than were the old, but as an historian he knows that men derive the articles of their faith from their reactions to the problems of their age. While he may appear cynical, he is not. Unlike Ratcliffe, Gore seeks to find a rational approach to the problems of modern life that will benefit all men.

Thus, of all the characters, Nathan Gore offers the clearest statement of a philosophy that could be called the satiric norm of the novel. Ratcliffe excites a grim laughter, somewhat like that of the modern black humor, for his gross deviations from the norm. The President causes laughter of a more tolerant kind because he seems somewhat the victim of his own stupidity. Carrington causes perhaps a smile because he does not have the courage to live without furtively trying to accommodate himself to the system. Even Madeleine Lee provokes a smile as she flirts with a system which she knows to be corrupt. But Gore has knowledge and character enough to make his point of view a standard by which others can be judged.

IV   *The Center of Revelation: Madeleine Lee*

From the standpoint of the construction of the novel, Adams's most important character is Madeleine Lee, who serves as the center of revelation. She is an intelligent woman of thirty who has had the experience of being married to a stockbroker, having had a child, and having survived them both.[18] She has money enough for her own wants and perhaps some for philanthropy, but she can no more believe in doing good than Emerson or Thoreau. She has read in philosophy and history and literature and still counts herself an ignorant person, but her curiosity does not turn in the direction of self-improvement. Instead, she turns to an area usually forbidden to women: "It was the feeling of a passenger on an ocean steamer whose mind will not give him rest until he has been in the engine-room and talked with the engineer. She wanted to see with her own eyes the action of primary forces, to touch with her own hand the massive machinery of society; to measure with her own mind the capacity of the motive power. She was bent upon getting to the heart of the great American mystery of democracy and government."[19] The natural inclination of a curiosity as strong as that of Mrs. Lee is to investigate the workings of the government in Washington. By allowing her to settle there, Adams stimulates his reader to identify his own curiosity with hers as she moves through a series of scenes in which the true nature of the workings of democracy is gradually revealed.

Mrs. Lee is first drawn to the Capitol, where she hopes for enlightenment from the speeches, especially in the Senate: "She wanted to learn how the machinery of government worked, and what was the quality of the men who controlled it. One by one, she passed them through her crucibles, and tested them by acids and by fire. A few survived her tests and came out alive, though more or less disfigured, where she had found impurities. Of the whole number, only one retained under this process enough character to interest her."[20] That one is Senator Ratcliffe from Illinois. A few days later she and her friend Carrington hear one of his speeches, about which Carrington comments, "See how he dodges all the sharp issues. What a thing it is to be a Yankee! What a genius the fellow has for leading a party!"[21] Ratcliffe's cleverness fascinates Mrs. Lee so much that she arranges to be introduced to him. She is clever enough to flatter him for his resemblance to Daniel Webster. She needs his good opinion, for "she wanted to understand this man; to turn him inside out; to experiment on him and use him as young physiologists use frogs and kittens. If there was good or bad in him, she meant to find its meaning."[22]

For all her determination, Mrs. Lee is slow to understand Ratcliffe. On the trip to Mount Vernon he has made clear that his is a philosophy of expediency—"If virtue won't answer our purpose, we must use vice."[23] But she has difficulty in accepting his admission at its full value, perhaps because she does not understand how deeply his will is corrupted. At the end of her trip to Mount Vernon she feels dissatisfied, but she is not at all sure of her bearings:

Was she, unknown to herself, gradually becoming tainted with the life about her? Or was Ratcliffe right in accepting the good and the bad together, and in being of his time since he was in it? Why was it, she said bitterly to herself, that everything Washington touched, he purified, even down to the associations of his house? and why is it that everything we touch seems soiled? Why do I feel unclean when I look at Mount Vernon? In spite of Mr. Ratcliffe, is it not better to be a child and to cry for the moon and stars?"[24]

Her tendency toward determinism makes her vulnerable to Ratcliffe's abilities as an actor. Ever since he lost his party's nomination for the Presidency to the Hoosier Quarryman, he has been maneuvering to become Secretary of the Treasury in order to secure control of the patronage as the means of becoming President. But he paints for Mrs. Lee a picture of a Cabinet arrayed against him and asks her whether or not he should accept the appointment anyway, from a sense of duty. She naively replies that he should do "whatever is most for the public good."[25] Ratcliffe tells her that he will accept, but that she must assume some responsibility for sending him into such a difficult situation. This appeal to her womanly desire for self-sacrifice blinds her to his corruption, though it enlightens her about the political corruption of others.

The scales begin to fall from Mrs. Lee's eyes when Carrington,

Ratcliffe's rival for her affections, suddenly receives an offer of a government assignment in Mexico. She cannot prove Ratcliffe's involvement, but she can see his motive, and she has been thoroughly exposed to manipulation and intrigue in politics. Because of this knowledge, she is ready to believe the message in the letter which Carrington has left for her to read in case she decides to marry Ratcliffe. The story of the bribe accepted by Ratcliffe shows that he is just as guilty of political corruption as are those he accused. The effect on Mrs. Lee's faith is devastating; not only has she seen that the public servants of democracy are corrupt, she knows that their corruption comes from the people themselves. Her final word in the novel shows how cynical she has become. Of her refusal to marry Ratcliffe, she says, "The bitterest part of this horrid story is that nine out of ten of our countrymen would say that I had made a mistake."[26]

V *Evaluation*

Although *Democracy* enjoyed a commercial success, it has never excited much critical acclaim. The reasons have more to do with the technical construction of the novel than with Adams's conception of the satire. He gives such small space to Nathan Gore that the character is easily overlooked. The reader then makes Madeleine Lee the embodiment of the satiric norm and misreads her disillusionment and cynicism for that of the novel and ultimately for that of Adams himself. Another technical difficulty is Adams's abuse of the omniscient point of view in editorializing, particularly about the motives of Ratcliffe. This disproportionate space for the analysis of villainy suggests that Adams had difficulty believing in what he saw. The effect is to compound the slighting of Gore and to reinforce in the reader's mind the impression of cynicism. But Adams was neither a cynic nor a determinist. The very act of writing *Democracy* proved his hope for the amelioration of the evils he castigated.

CHAPTER 6

Esther

ADAMS'S second novel, *Esther,* appeared in 1884 under the pseudonym "Frances Snow Compton." Adams had fixed on the rather quixotic idea of experimenting on a release of the novel without any of the usual publisher's notices or advertisements so as to see what the drawing power of the novel itself would be. With his experience of the power of publicity in numerous political campaigns he had witnessed, he could hardly have been in much doubt about the outcome. The book sold very poorly, and Adams professed to be disappointed. But he did not reveal the secret of its publication, which became known only at the time of his death.

Adams's novel is frequently interpreted as a dramatization of the conflict between science and religion, but very little of the action stems from this problem because the conflict is never far from resolution. Much more important is the problem of determinism and freedom of choice: the tendency of institutions to confine at the same time as they support, and the difficulty even the free spirit has in liberating one caught by the institution. Adams's theme is not very far from that of *Democracy,* where Ratcliffe, potentially a good man, is deprived of his freedom by political institutions, yet is beyond rescue by Madeleine Lee. In *Esther* Adams's irony is less bitter because Stephen Hazard is a slave to the church, but Esther Dudley fails in her attempt to rescue him just as surely as Madeleine Lee failed in the earlier novel.

I *Stephen Hazard, Churchman*

The aesthetic qualities of the new church of St. John's on Fifth Avenue in New York City come sharply to the reader's attention in the opening scene of *Esther.* Although the frescoes are still unfinished, they give the effect of "autumn gardens" or of "October woods," and their splendor is matched by the splendor of the sun's

illumination of the crimson and green in the stained-glass figure of
St. John. Yet these splendors looked down upon "a display of human
vanities that would have called out a vehement Lamentation of
Jeremiah or Song of Solomon, had these poets been present in flesh
as they were in figure."[1]

The young minister, Stephen Hazard, performs his ritualistic
functions so well that some of his audience comment on his his-
trionic abilities. And in his sermon he shows no humility at all:

He took possession of his flock with a general advertisement that he owned
every sheep in it, white or black, and to show that there could be no doubt
on the matter, he added a general claim to the right of property in all
mankind and the universe. He did this in the name and on behalf of the
church universal, but there was self-assertion in the quiet air with which he
pointed out the nature of his title, and then, after sweeping all human
thought and will into his strong-box, shut down the lid with a sharp click,
and bade his audience kneel.[2]

He makes unrestricted claims for the church: "The hymns of David,
the plays of Shakespeare, the metaphysics of Descartes, the crimes
of Borgia, the virtues of Antonine, the atheism of yesterday and the
materialism of today, were all emanations of divine thought, doing
their appointed work."[3] Even science can no longer cause the
church concern, for the church now knows that she and science
must both begin with the simple consciousness of existence. The
irony of this line of reasoning is that Hazard's audience cannot follow
it; they would prefer a justification on the basis of materialism.

His lack of realism is emphasized by Professor Strong, who has
known him over a period of time: "I thought if he came here he
would find that he had no regular community to deal with but just
an Arab horde, and that it was nonsense to talk of saving the souls of
New Yorkers who have no souls to be saved. But he thought it his
duty to take the offer. Aunt Sarah hit it right when she called him a
Christian martyr in the amphitheater. At college, we used to call
him St. Stephen. He had this same idea that the church was every
thing, and that every thing belonged to the church."[4] Even though a
person like this is very far removed from the reality of the ordinary
parishioner, he can continue to exist because of the protective nature of the institution, which is set up for just such a purpose.

Although a man like Hazard might seem free because of his

capacity to lead his congregation, Adams shows him a prisoner: "In a large library, with book-cases to the ceiling, and books lying in piles on the floor; with pictures, engravings and etchings leaning against the books and the walls, and every sort of literary encumbrance scattered in the way of heedless feet; in the midst of confusion confounded, Mr. Hazard was stretched on a sofa trying to read, but worn out by fatigue and excitement."[5] His intellectual confinement is symbolized by the books around him, which encompass many fields: divinity, classics, poetry, novels, illustrated works of art, and even music. Of course, the church requires of him many other duties, some of which are much less pleasant than reading. Adams describes a meeting of a church committee at which a parishioner speaks for two hours on the question of the kitchen range and the plumbing at the children's hospital. Though Hazard is not present, the committee votes to have him on its visiting committee. When he is next seen carrying out his duty at the hospital, he is described as "miserable with a cold, and very weak with fatigue. His next sermon was turning out dull and disjointed. His building committee was interfering and quarreling with Wharton. A harsh north-west wind had set his teeth on edge and filled his eyes with dust. Rarely had he found himself in a less spiritual frame of mind than when he entered this room."[6]

But the intellectual and social pressures are dwarfed by the spiritual, as Adams explains:

The strain of standing in a pulpit is great. No human being ever yet constructed was strong enough to offer himself long as a light to humanity without showing the effect on his constitution. Buddhist saints stand for years silent, on one leg, or with arms raised above their heads, but the limbs shrivel and the mind shrivels with the limbs. Christian saints have found it necessary from time to time to drop their arms and to walk on their legs, but they do it with a sort of apology or defiance, and sometimes do it, if they can, by stealth. One is a saint or one is not; every man can choose the career that suits him; but to be saint and sinner at the same time requires singular ingenuity. For this reason, wise clergymen, whose tastes, though in themselves innocent, may give scandal to others, enjoy their relaxation, so far as they can, in privacy.[7]

The tension of such restraints can only naturally provoke a desire for release.

II *Esther Dudley, Free Spirit*

Esther Dudley, though she has not been brought up in the church, is present at the first service at St. John's and is obviously attracted to the minister. Though her cousin calls her "the sternest little Pagan I know,"[8] Stephen Hazard is interested in her opinion of his sermon. Hearing that she wonders whether or not he believes all that he said, he declares that her question is the one he wishes all his congregation would ask. Perhaps there is a good deal of irony, both conscious and unconscious, in his remark. Esther's freedom allows Hazard to think of his own orthodoxy, but it may also produce in him a desire for freedom as well.

Certain it is that she catches his imagination enough for him to ask the painter Wharton to explain her type. Wharton describes her as "one of the most marked American types I ever saw."[9] Her physical appearance shows a lack of concern for the opinions of fashion: she is too thin and she sometimes dresses badly. But Wharton says of her nonetheless,

Miss Dudley interests me. I want to know what she can make of life. She gives one the idea of a lightly-sparred yacht in mid-ocean; unexpected; you ask yourself what the devil she is doing there. She sails gayly along, though there is no land in sight and plenty of rough weather coming. She never read a book, I believe, in her life. She tries to paint, but she is only a second rate amateur and will never be anything more, though she has done one or two things which I give you my word I would like to have done myself. She picks up all she knows without an effort and knows nothing well, yet she seems to understand whatever is said. Her mind is as irregular as her face, and both have the same peculiarity. I notice that the lines of her eyebrows, nose and mouth all end with a slight upward curve like a yacht's sails, which gives a kind of hopefulness and self-confidence to her expression. Mind and face have the same curves.[10]

Her spirit, Wharton thinks, is not medieval but pagan, and her presence makes him painfully aware of the failure of the church.

Despite Esther's seeming disqualifications for the task of painting church murals, she is engaged to paint St. Cecilia in St. John's with Catherine Brooke, a young visitor from Colorado, as her model.[11] Hazard lectures her on early Christian art, but she can feel no sympathy for drawing the attenuated figures that he feels would be proper. She listens politely, but paints according to her own understanding. Wharton soon notices that Hazard is allowing Esther more freedom than he does the other painters. All the other murals have depicted gaunt figures, to which Esther objects that they give the church no heart. They are merely theater, she says, and Wharton agrees. She and Catherine want to make St. Cecilia an attractive, warm figure, but they can do so only by making her clash with the tone of the church. Eventually, though, Esther becomes dissatisfied with her painting and wishes Wharton to improve it. But he tells her that he cannot paint innocence as she has done, because he is no longer innocent.

During all this time Hazard has been making it more and more clear that he is not so much interested in St. Cecilia as in her painter. Esther, understanding her own unsuitability to be the wife of a clergyman, removes herself from him as much as possible. But when her father dies, she becomes more vulnerable to Hazard's affection and she soon finds herself engaged.

III *Flight*

No sooner is Esther engaged to him than Stephen Hazard preaches a sermon into which he cleverly insinuates material about their personal relationship.[12] To Esther, with her ideas of individual freedom, this represents an invasion of her rights, though Hazard, accustomed to submerging himself in the church, would not think so. Suddenly aware of their differences in outlook, Esther tries to read theology in order to understand Hazard's point of view. And she consults with her cousin Dr. Strong, the professor of paleontology, who assures her that religion and science are alike in requiring faith. But when he half-jestingly offers her a crucifix as a formula for the reduction of her pride, he sees that she is indeed serious about her problem.

Both the lovers think of escape as a way out of their problem. Hazard suggests that they go to Japan and paint, and Esther eagerly agrees.[13] Then he repents of his idea and tries to convince Esther that she should not be concerned with the parish gossip about their philosophical differences. Esther is unconvinced and leaves for Niagara Falls.[14] Hazard soon follows. Both are susceptible to the natural beauty of the setting, but his disagreement with her interpretation of some paintings of the falls suggests the difference still between them. She continues to find her greatest security in her freedom to choose. His, on the other hand, comes from his faith in the protectiveness of institutions, for which he willingly gives up the right to choose. Esther is right in her opinion that she and the church would be competitors and that she would lose eventually. So she regretfully turns away, admitting that she still loves him.

IV   *Evaluation*

R. P. Blackmur thinks that *Democracy* and *Esther* are about on a par, suffering equally from Adams's weaknesses as a novelist.[15] Yet it is difficult not to see *Esther* as the lesser work. Adams was always interested in politics, and the sharpness of some of the pictures in *Democracy* makes the reader feel his interest. The scene in which the President and his wife are standing like puppets in a receiving line at the White House is memorable for its irony. But *Esther* has no scene of comparable force, because Adams did not feel the problems of the church with anything like the urgency he felt those of politics. If Hazard is imprisoned by an institution that has relatively little vitality, then he seems merely weak. Though Esther has a much stronger character than he, her concern for him ultimately makes her seem less consequential than she ought. Both *Esther* and *Democracy*, then, are interesting less in themselves than in what they show about the intellectual development of Henry Adams.

CHAPTER 7

The History

UNLIKE Edward Gibbon, Adams left unrecorded the circumstances in which the idea for his *History of the United States During the Administrations of Thomas Jefferson and James Madison* originated. In all likelihood his inspiration came not in a flash but in the slow expansion of his interest during his research for the Gallatin volumes. Before their publication he was already planning a European trip to gather materials for the projected history, a labor which occupied much of 1879 and 1880.[1] Four years later he had completed two volumes, which he had privately printed to facilitate correction. His plans for their publication and for completion of the other projected volumes were interrupted by the suicide of Marian Hooper Adams in 1885.[2] He spent part of the following year on a trip to Japan with John LaFarge.[3] Returning to the *History* with his usual energy, he occupied himself with its publication between 1889 and 1891. Although he had taken particular pains to make his narrative readable, the public no longer read history as avidly as in the days of Gibbon or Macaulay or even Parkman. Though his impact on the general public was small, his history brought him the respect of the specialists, a respect which he continues to hold.

Adams might easily have called his work a history of the United States during the Napoleonic era, for his interpretation stressed the strong influence on American life of events in Europe during the early nineteenth century. It was one of the ironies of history that Napoleon became First Consul in 1799, not quite a year before Jefferson was elected President. Each was brought to power by the operation of democratic forces in his country, yet each ultimately took a course diametrically opposed to the other. Jefferson came to office with the firm intention of reducing government to the vanishing point. He sought to keep military expenditures low, but he

69

soon found himself frustrated, in part because of the influence of Napoleon on the peace of Europe. In Adams's interpretation of the presidencies of Jefferson and Madison, three events took on supreme importance: the Louisiana Purchase, the Embargo, and the War of 1812. All of these showed the strong influence of Napoleon, who for Adams was the villain of the piece. Though Adams includes the details of much unnecessary suffering, his story emerges as very nearly a comedy. Despite the follies of the political leaders of America and of Europe, the United States moved out of the Napoleonic period in better condition than when it began. Neither Jefferson's vacillation about the constitutional question of the Louisiana Purchase nor Madison's cowering in the woods during the burning of Washington could obscure the vitality of a democratic people engrossed in the development of its new land.

I   *America in 1800*

Adams's opening chapter on "Physical and Economical Conditions" dwells on the theme of the enormous size and the undeveloped condition of the country in 1800. With less than one-fifth the population of France, the country had to find resources to provide the means of life for a people scattered over a huge and unfriendly territory. Adams comments that "among the numerous difficulties with which the Union was to struggle, the disproportion between the physical obstacles and the material means for overcoming them was one of the most striking."[4] Manufacturing of essential goods was done on too small a scale; farming practices were poor; housing in many parts of the country was hardly better than in the days of Charlemagne; and transportation was impeded by lack of internal improvements. The cities were small and capital was scarce. There was great hope for centers like Charleston, South Carolina, but in most of the country the chance for development seemed remote.

In order to examine the intellectual and social condition of the country in 1800, Adams divides it into three sections: New England, the Middle States, and the South. The first he found to be a conservative section, which still looked to England as the source of its intellectual life. Although the Congregational clergy was respected, it was declining in influence. Timothy Dwight, John Trumbull, and Joel Barlow were among those who gave the section some literary pretensions, though they, too, looked backward to the eighteenth century for inspiration. Adams comments that this extreme conservatism left no room for development along the lines already set down. The weakness of its leadership made the section especially vulnerable to the changes already beginning to be evident in Europe.

The Middle States did not have the high moral tone of New England, but they had greater flexibility to deal with the problems of a developing country. Pennsylvania was the only truly democratic state; it is for Adams "the ideal American State, easy, tolerant, and contented."[5] New England did not particularly admire the intellect of Pennsylvania, but the state seemed effective in obtaining its ends. In literature it had produced Philip Freneau, H. H. Brackenridge, and Alexander Wilson, all democrats. Its social institutions, too, excelled: even the insane were given attention under the humanitarian and democratic outlook fostered by the state.

The southern states were far more rural and therefore more isolated and provincial than their northern neighbors. Jefferson, the most important thinker of the section, believed that an agricultural economy was preferable for the South to one devoted to manufacturing. His Virginia and Kentucky Resolutions, asserting states' rights over those of the federal government, were perhaps the greatest political expression of the belief in isolation. But these ideas were not susceptible of further development. Nor was the rest of the South much more productive. Charleston was the only sizable urban center in the entire section, but it had to exert its influence over a large, unfriendly territory. The backwoods region was a bastion of conservatism; its greatest spokesman was John C. Calhoun. He was an anachronism who would have been well suited for New England a hundred years before, but in 1800 he was merely an obstacle to development.

In the chapter "American Ideals," Adams offers an interpretation of the American character as it stood at the beginning of its national life. Everywhere it was optimistic, convinced of its vigor as opposed to the decrepitude of Europe. The American's ignorance of Europe was returned by misunderstanding. Even a poet like Wordsworth showed an unnecessary hostility to the American. An attitude like this came partly from the American's deeply ingrained idealism, which made no effort to be understood. Like Jefferson the typical American believed so firmly in the doctrine of progress that he could hardly stop to notice some of the problems of his faith: the question of moral progress was particularly troublesome to the New Englander, because Jefferson seemed to assume that it would come with physical and intellectual progress. Whatever its theoretical position, Adams feels, the task facing it was of such a nature that the theory would have to be equal to the remaking of the American as a higher part of the human race.

II   *The Louisiana Purchase*

Adams puts great stress on the character of Jefferson as the strongest influence on the government which took control from the Federalists in 1801. Concealing none of his distaste for some of Jefferson's characteristics, he nonetheless manages to convey a sense of the greatness of the man as well. Jefferson is for Adams a doctrinaire idealist: he was absolutely unswerving in his faith in all of mankind. Yet he could carry his theories to ludicrous extremes. A good example was his manner of dress. To show his contempt for fashion, he dressed so carelessly as President as to offend foreign dignitaries who were unaware of the point Jefferson was trying to make. A greater sensitivity to the feelings or ordinary mankind would have enabled him to implement his theories more effectively.

Adams's analysis of the inaugural address reveals some of the contradictions in the man. Jefferson thought of the election of 1800 as a revolution in which the monarchical Federalists were defeated by his own advocates of true democracy. But he sought to placate the Federalists with the expression, "We are all Republicans, we are all Federalists."[6] And he paid the Federalist administrations the compliment of declaring that they had kept the government free and firm. Adams comments: "Clearly, Jefferson credited government with strength which belonged to society; and if he meant to practice upon this idea, by taking the tone of 'the strongest government on earth' in the face of Bonaparte and Pitt, whose governments were strong in a different sense, he might properly have developed this idea at more length, for it was likely to prove deeply interesting."[7] Jefferson had written three years earlier, in drafting the Kentucky Resolutions, that the proper remedy for a state abused by the federal government was nullification. But in his inaugural address he stressed the need for "absolute acquiescence in the decisions of the majority." If Jefferson sounded conciliatory to the Federalists in his inaugural address, he did not seem so in his private correspondence of the period. Adams does not directly accuse Jefferson of duplicity, but he makes it obvious that Jefferson seems to him less than honest. The attitudes of the second and sixth Presidents die hard in the latest Adams.

Yet in summarizing the character of Jefferson, Adams pays tribute to its complexity: "A few broad strokes of the brush," he said, "would paint the portraits of all the early Presidents with this exception."[8] But "Jefferson could be painted only touch by touch, with a fine pencil, and the perfection of the likeness depended upon the shifting and uncertain flicker of its semi-transparent shadows."[9] Then he quotes Hamilton to show that while Jefferson carried the reputation of a zealot, he had impressed Hamilton as one who would temporize.[10] Hamilton attributed this quality to Jefferson's egotism, but Adams finds Jefferson far too complex to be delineated by a simple formula.

Across the Atlantic, seemingly in a world completely apart from that of Jefferson, another genius was head of state. Though he, as much as Jefferson, was the product of the revolutionary forces that swept the final quarter of the eighteenth century, for Adams, he bears no likeness to the American president:

Most picturesque of all figures in modern history, Napoleon Bonaparte, like Milton's Satan on his throne of state, although surrounded by a group of figures less striking than himself, sat unapproachable on his bad eminence; or, when he moved, the dusky air felt an unusual weight. His conduct was often mysterious, and sometimes so arbitrary as to seem insane; . . . ambition that ground its heel into every obstacle; restlessness that often defied common-sense; selfishness that eat like a cancer into his reasoning faculties; energy such as had never before been combined with equal genius and resources; ignorance that would have amused a schoolboy; and a moral sense which regarded truth and falsehood as equally useful modes of expression.[11]

Just as the genius of Jefferson attracted a disciple in Gallatin, so the genius of Bonaparte was served in foreign affairs by Talleyrand. Each leader was thereby provided with reinforcement both of a psychological and practical kind.

A strange set of circumstances brought these men into direct confrontation. Though France had given up her colonies on the North American continent before the American Revolution, she continued her interests in the West Indies. During the French Revolution, the blacks of Santo Domingo, under the leadership of

Toussaint L'Ouverture, rebelled.[12] For some years he remained in effective control. But Napoleon determined to reassert the rights of France over her possession, and in 1802 he sent out to the colony an army which was surprisingly successful. Toussaint was captured and sent to France a prisoner, where he died. But the troubles in the colony did not cease with victory. Because supplies and men were so rapidly consumed in this endeavor, Napoleon was unable to send the force he had intended to establish French ascendancy in Louisiana.[13]

Adams examines in great detail the capricious moves of Napoleon during the negotiations for the Louisiana Purchase. First, he dwells on the suddenness with which Napoleon decided to sell Louisiana. Months of entreaty by the American Commission had failed to get a response; then on April 10, 1803, Napoleon called in two of his ministers to explain his plan to cede the territory to the United States. He considered the colony already lost, for he expected England to seize it. Then Adams adds the famous scene in the bath, where his brothers Lucien and Joseph went to dissuade Napoleon from selling so cheaply this valuable possession. The fierce altercation, Napoleon's falling back into the water so as to splash his brother, the thrown snuffbox—the Napoleonic renunciation of the support of his brothers—all bespoke the childishly overdeveloped will of the man. Adams underscores the importance of the act: "The sale of Louisiana was the turning point in Napoleon's career; no true Frenchman forgave it. A second betrayal of France, it announced to his fellow conspirators that henceforward he alone was to profit by the treason of the 18th Brumaire."[14] Though Adams may be exaggerating the importance of the sale of Louisiana for Napoleon's career, his analysis of its psychological importance has merit: "It is reasonable to believe that the depths of his nature concealed a wish to hide forever the monument of a defeat. As he would have liked to blot Corsica, Egypt, and Santo Domingo from the map, and wipe from human memory the record of his failures, he may have taken pleasure in flinging Louisiana far off, and burying it forever from the sight of France in the bosom of the only government which could absorb and conceal it."[15]

If the sale of Louisiana made difficulties for Napoleon, its purchase made as many for Jefferson. He had moved quickly to buy Louisiana because he recognized that such an opportunity might well never come again. But he was also a strict constructionist of the

Constitution, and he could find no authorization in that document for the addition of territory to the nation. Believing a constitutional amendment necessary, he drew up a proposal that would have divided the Louisiana territory at the thirty-second parallel so as to confirm Indian ownership of the land north of that line. But he could interest no one in this proposal nor in any other. Finally he gave up the effort, but not without warning that the admission of Louisiana made blank paper of the Constitution[16] and that the treaty-making power could supersede all written law. Adams agrees that Jefferson was right about both points and that the purchase of Louisiana made obsolete the strict construction of the Constitution.

In the debate in Congress about the admission of Louisiana, no enthusiasm arose for the idea of an amendment to the Constitution; Senator John Quincy Adams could not even obtain a second for his motion to amend. A simple bill in Congress sufficed, which Adams describes as "an act of sovereignty as despotic as the corresponding acts of France and Spain."[17] The bill for governing the territory made no attempt to extend the guarantees of the Constitution to its inhabitants, a fact about which Adams comments ironically: "Louisiana received a government in which its people, who had been solemnly promised all the rights of American citizens, were set apart, not as citizens, but as subjects lower in the political scale than the meanest tribes of Indians, whose right to self-government was never questioned."[18] Much later South Carolina was to complain in justifying secession that the country had transferred powers from the states to the central government, which had thereby become despotic. Adams suggests that it was the Southerners who had bypassed the constitutional question in 1803 and had thereby brought their difficulties upon themselves.

One of the most important themes of Adams's *History* is the assimilation of Federalist principles by Jefferson's Republicans. Of the many incidents described in Adams's voluminous narrative, those concerning the Louisiana Purchase illustrate best the political situation at the beginning of Jefferson's Presidency. Though Adams may be suspected of trying to vindicate the second President, he does not seem to regard the triumph of Federalism as inevitable. Instead, he constantly deplores the yielding of the Jeffersonian principles to expediency. No mere determinist, he would agree with Sir Isaiah Berlin in feeling it his duty to comment on the weaknesses of his historical subjects.[19]

III *The Embargo*

Adams's pages are thickly crowded with people and events of the middle years of Jefferson's two terms in office. None is more interesting than Aaron Burr as a study in human eccentricity. But neither he nor Monroe nor John Randolph had the ability to affect the course of the entire country as much as Jefferson himself. Particularly in the series of events called "The Embargo," which marked the close of his second term of office, Jefferson's character made itself felt throughout the nation.

Although Jefferson's commitment to a small military budget presumed an ability to stay out of war, he was unlucky in that American interests so often impinged on those of France and England. To maintain a neutral position between them was nearly impossible. After the battle of Trafalgar in 1805 England was supreme on the ocean, but Napoleon was still master of the European continent. Despite the deficiencies of his sea-power, he sought to regain some advantage on the ocean by issuing, on November 21, 1806, the Berlin Decree.[20] This document proclaimed a blockade of England and forbade all trade with her. At about the same time Monroe was in England trying to negotiate a treaty that would improve commercial relations between the Americans and the British and that would remove the problem of the impressment of seamen from American ships.[21] But the treaty was so weak that Jefferson refused to present it to the Senate. The situation of the United States at the end of 1806 was that of a weakling caught between the upper and the lower millstones with no prospect of easy extrication.

The next year saw relations with the English steadily worsen. First, the American ship *Chesapeake* suffered an outrageous attack by the British ship *Leopard*.[22] Hearing that English deserters were a part of the crew of the *Chesapeake,* the British admiral issued orders for any ship of his command to stop her. The *Leopard* apprehended her setting out to sea, went through the formalities of demanding the release of the men, and then attacked the American ship, which was unprepared for battle. The *Chesapeake* was forced to strike her colors and go back to port. The high-handedness of the British, especially distasteful because only one English sailor had been aboard, produced a great furor in the American public.

A second outrage was the Order in Council of November 11, 1807. This was essentially the British response to Napoleon's Berlin

Decree. Its provisions, as Adams says, were simple: "Any American vessel carrying any cargo was liable to capture if it sailed for any port in Europe from which the British flag was excluded. In other words, American commerce was made English."[23] Even the British expected that war would be likely to follow. But the problem for America was that she had cause for war against both belligerents. Even if she chose one or the other, she was poorly prepared because of the policy of the Jefferson administration toward military expenditures. More important, the United States was a small, poor, agricultural nation which did not have the resources to do battle with two of the most powerful military establishments on earth.

Adams is much less sympathetic to Jefferson's pacifist point of view than some later scholars have been. Adams depicts Jefferson as a man obsessed:

So confident was Jefferson in his theory of peaceable coercion that he would hardly have thought his administrative career complete, had he quitted office without being allowed to prove the value of his plan. The fascination which it exercised over his mind was quite as much due to temperament as to logic; for if reason told him that Europe could be starved into concession, temperament added another motive still more alluring. If Europe persisted in her conduct America would still be safe, and all the happier for cutting off connection with countries where violence and profligacy ruled supreme.[24]

Adams further illustrates Jefferson's pacific nature by quoting from a letter to a grandson in which he advised the young man to avoid fiery zealots in politics "as you would an angry bull."[25] Adams plays on Jefferson's figure:

As President of the United States, Jefferson was bent upon carrying out the plan of keeping within himself; but the bull of which he spoke as unfit for a man of sense to dispute with, and which he saw filling the whole path before him, was not only angry, but mad with pain and blind with rage; his throat and flanks were torn and raw where the Corsican wolf had set his teeth; a pack of mastiffs and curs were baiting him and yelling at his heels, and his bood-shot eyes no longer knew friend from foe, as he rushed with a roar of stupid rage directly upon the President.[26]

But Jefferson saw only the opportunity to please his friends by experimenting with the doctrine of peaceable coercion. And because he had so carefully managed the Treasury, he had almost no

opposition. Less than two months after Jefferson called Congress
into session, he signed the bill for the Embargo.

Although certain sections of the country benefited from the diminution of imports and therefore favored Jefferson's policy, Adams's
account stresses its negative aspects. The shipping of New England
was hard hit and many citizens tried to defy the customs officers.
The coastal trade seemed to be outside the provisions of the act, but
smuggling soon became a problem. Jefferson did not hesitate to
enforce the law, even to the point of bloodshed. Once again Adams
writes with irony of Jefferson's swing to the right:

That President Jefferson should exercise "dangerous and odious" powers,
carrying the extremest principles of his Federalist predecessors to their
extremest results; that he should in doing so invite bloodshed, strain his
military resources, quarrel with the State authorities of his own party and
with judges whom he had himself made; that he should depend for constitutional law on Federalist judges whose doctrines he had hitherto believed
fatal to liberty,—these were the first fruits of the Embargo.[27]

In a chapter which seems callous to those who have experienced
the bloodshed of the twentieth century, Adams writes a comparative
study of the cost of war as opposed to the Embargo. The harm done
to the Constitution was about equal, he judges. The economic effects of both were harmful. But the harm done by the Embargo in
corrupting men was much greater: gambling and speculation prolif-
erated and the rich became richer at the expense of the poor. But,
on the other hand,

if war made men brutal, at least it made them strong; it called out the
qualities best fitted to survive in the struggle for existence. To risk life for
one's country was no mean act even when done for selfish motives; and to
die that others might more happily live was the highest act of self-sacrifice
to be reached by man. War, with all its horrors, could purify as well as
debase; it dealt with high motives and vast interests; taught courage, discipline, and stern sense of duty. Jefferson must have asked himself in vain
what lessons of heroism or duty were taught by his system of peaceable
coercion, which turned every citizen into an enemy of the laws,—preaching
the fear of war and of self-sacrifice, making many smugglers and traitors, but
not a single hero.[28]

Ironically, in this passage Adams, usually clear-eyed, allows his social Darwinism to blind him so that he becomes more theoretical than Jefferson himself.

One of the greatest losses brought by the Embargo was the decline in the personal popularity of Jefferson.[29] He left office almost as unpopular as John Adams. In one of his last appointments, that of William Short to the Ministry at St. Petersburg, he was rebuffed by the unanimous vote of the Senate. But even worse, perhaps, was his inability to keep the Embargo alive until he left office; just three days before the expiration of his term, he signed the bill which repealed the Embargo and thus ended his dream of peaceful coercion.

IV *The War of 1812*

If Adams registers disgust with the attempts of Jefferson to steer between France and England, he can do no better for Madison. The chapter headings "Executive Weakness," "Legislative Impotence," and "Incapacity of Government" suggest his mood. The penuriousness of the Jefferson administrations about military expenditures was continued under Madison; both the navy and the army were so weak as to be of no use in negotiations with the great European powers. The navy had been the victim of Jefferson's gunboat scheme, by which a great deal of money had been spent on small boats armed with only one gun.[30] In practice, these boats had proved worse than useless because they had cost a great deal to maintain without performing any effective service. The army was in worse condition because of the weakness of its officer corps. Its inefficiency was demonstrated by the loss of 764 troops to disease in the first year out of the 2,000 sent to guard New Orleans. Most of these deaths could have been prevented had General Wilkinson obeyed the orders of the Secretary of War.[31] Even the Treasury Department, which had been the mainstay of Jefferson's administrations, was showing the effect of the Non-Intercourse Act of March 1, 1809; its surplus had turned into a deficit. And while the American government seemed to grow weaker, the power of Napoleon was being enhanced by his military victories. His supremacy on the European continent and that of England on the sea boded no good for an America nearly stripped of any power of retaliation.

Adams reserves some of his most cutting sarcasm for the legislative branch: "No course would have pleased Congress so much as to do nothing at all; but this wish could not be fully gratified."[32] The

Senate occupied itself with a resolution sponsored by William
Branch Giles of Virginia to censure the conduct of the British minister to the United States, Francis James Jackson. Again Adams writes
bitingly:

No episode in the national history was less encouraging than the conduct of
Congress in regard to Giles's Resolution. From December 18 to January 4,
the House wasted its time and strength in proving the helplessness of
Executive, Congress, parties, and people in the grasp of Europe. With
painful iteration every Republican proved that the nation had been insulted
by the British minister; while every Federalist protested his inability to
discern the insult, and his conviction that no insult was intended. Except as
preliminary to measures of force, Giles's Resolution showed neither dignity
nor object; yet the Republicans embarrassed themselves with denials of the
Federalist charge that such language toward a foreign government must
have a warlike motive, while the Federalists insisted that their interests
required peace.[33]

Instead of seeking measures to increase the efficiency of the army
and navy, Congress voted to reduce both establishments. Adams
castigates their attitude:

Meanwhile nothing could be more dangerous to the Americans than the loss
of self-respect. The habit of denouncing themselves as cowards and of
hearing themselves denounced as a race that cared only for money tended
to produce the qualities imputed. Americans of 1810 were persuaded that
they could not meet Englishmen or Frenchmen on equal terms, man
against man, or stand in battle against the veterans of Napoleon or Nelson.
The sense of national and personal inferiority sank astonishingly deep.
Reasonable enough as regarded the immense superiority of Europe in organization, it passed bounds when it condemned everything American as
contemptible, or when the Federalist gentry refused to admit the Democrats of Pennsylvania or the Republicans of Virginia or the Government of
Washington into the circle of civilized life.[34]

Undoubtedly Adams's old-fashioned idealism would have been better understood by the early nineteenth century than by the latter
twentieth; but no matter how much one was devoted to the idea of
the heroic, he must have been restrained by practical considerations. Adams, despite his reputation with some scholars as a determinist, believes so much in the heroic that he thinks his David could
smite two Goliaths at once.

At long last, in 1811, the country developed the mood for war. But Adams is still sardonic: "A passion that needed to be nursed for five years before it acquired strength to break into act, could not seem genuine to men who did not share it. A nation which had submitted to robbery and violence in 1805, in 1807, in 1809, could not readily lash itself into rage in 1811 when it had no new grievance to allege; nor could the public feel earnest in maintaining national honor, for every one admitted that the nation had sacrificed its honor, and must fight to regain it."[35] Yet practical considerations seemed to rise in the public consciousness: for the first time impressments were given their true place as the most imperative reasons for war. By the end of 1811 a new Congress had been seated which contained a group of young men who were bent on war with England. Among them were Henry Clay, John C. Calhoun, and Felix Grundy.[36] Because they were interested in the conquest of Canada, they pushed through Congress a bill to increase the strength of the army. But their efforts made relatively little headway because of the inefficiency of the regular units, and they paid no attention at all to the navy. The state of military preparedness at the beginning of 1812 was still far from acceptable.

The timing of the declaration of war gives Adams another opportunity for irony: The Orders in Council, which had been so obnoxious to the Americans, were repealed on June 17, 1812; the next day the United States declared war; and two days later Napoleon issued the first bulletin of his Grand Army on the eve of his invasion of Russia.[37] The British concession might have given the Americans pause. But acting in concert with Napoleon seemed in their own best interest, for no one could have foreseen the disaster which awaited Napoleon's army. What had seemed good fortune in the summer turned to ill by winter, and a floundering America found itself facing an angered England suddenly free of its worst menace.

If Adams inclined to war as a remedy for the faults of policy in the American government, he did not like the kind of war Madison's government was able to wage. Even before the declaration of war, preparations had gone forward to secure the western territories. But the first incident after war was declared, Adams remarks, "told the story of the campaign."[38] The American mail service was so slow that the British commander knew about the declaration two days before General Hull of the American army received his despatch. The Secretary of War ordered Hull to invade Canada, but his movements were ill coordinated with those of the other American forces along the Canadian border. Eventually Hull was besieged at Detroit and was obliged to surrender his entire force. At the same time Fort Dearborn at Chicago was burned, and the entire Northwest was lost to the British and Indians.[39]

The navy was poorly equipped at the beginning of the war, having only sixteen seagoing vessels of war. But the skill of American seamen helped to save the day. The *Constitution* demonstrated their abilities when she managed, though becalmed, to escape from five British ships. It became obvious that the next test would be more decisive, and Adams comments: "For once, even the Federalists of New England felt their blood stir; for their own President and their own votes had called these frigates into existence, and a victory won by the *Constitution*, which had been built by their hands, was in their eyes a greater victory over their political opponents than over the British."[40] Happily for them, the *Constitution* next encountered the *Guerrière*, whose captain showed such arrogance that he allowed himself to be completely overwhelmed by the fighting spirit of the Americans.[41] The sinking of the *Guerrière* and the capture of the *Macedonian* were only two of the more brilliant exploits of the navy in the first months of the war. And about all of them Adams writes with obvious sectional and family pride.

The usual inefficiency of the American government marked the logistical arrangements of the later campaigns in the West. Adams describes the disorganization surrounding the supply of equipment to the forces commanded by William Henry Harrison:

Universal confusion, want of oversight and organization, added to physical difficulties, gave play to laziness, incapacity, and dishonesty. No bills of lading were used; no accounts were kept with the wagoners; and the teams were valued so high, on coming into service, that the owners were willing to destroy them for the price to be received. The waste of government funds was appalling, for nothing short of a million rations at the Maumee Rapids could serve Harrison's objects, and after two months of effort not a ration had been carried within fifty miles of the spot.[42]

With so much inefficiency in the American forces, the British needed little to insure victory. Their triumph at the River Raisin brought fame and promotion to their General Procter, whom Adams considers "the most favorable event of the war for the American armies he was to meet."[43]

Unfortunately, the American generals in Canada were even worse. General Dearborn made an expedition against York, the capital of Upper Canada, which had no military value. Some soldiers burned, without authorization, the public buildings, a deed which was later used to justify the burning of the Capitol at Washington.[44] An accidental explosion of a powder magazine made this battle one of the bloodiest of the war. Then disaster followed disaster until Madison was forced to consent to Dearborn's retirement.[45] In the operations against Montreal, a conflict of personalities between General Wilkinson and General Hampton and the failure of the Secretary of War to coordinate the campaign caused operations to falter short of their goal. Again Adams remarks, sardonically: "The only happy result of the campaign was to remove all the older generals—Wilkinson, Hampton, and Morgan Lewis—from active service."[46]

Despite the early successes of the navy, the British established a blockade of the American coast, with crippling effect on the economy by 1813.[47] All efforts to break the blockade availed nothing. Worse, the navy suffered the disgraceful loss of both the *Chesapeake*[48] and the *Argus*[49] to boarding parties from their British opponents. But in the use of privateers the Americans were more successful: they established a blockade of the British Isles and did more to bring about a desire for peace among English merchants than did the regular navy. Yet Adams notes that here, too, the system operated very inefficiently: "Like all gambling ventures, privateering was not profitable."[50] More than half the privateers never took a prize, and their competition for experienced crews made recruitment for the navy difficult. The government, Adams thought, would have done better to keep all military operations in its own hands.

After the recovery of Detroit in 1813, the battles in the North went somewhat better for the Americans, particularly because of naval operations on the Great Lakes. In July 1814 the Americans won the battle of Chippewa, which Adams assesses: "Never again after that combat was an army of American regulars beaten by British troops. Small as the affair was, and unimportant in military results, it gave to the United States army a character and pride it had never before possessed."[51] The Americans fought well at Lundy's Lane and Fort Erie; but the British, relieved of the pressure of Napoleon, began to send large numbers of reinforcements to

Canada. Once again, the American leadership compromised what had been done: General Izard gave up his position and went into winter quarters on October 21. Fort Erie was abandoned and military activity in that sector ceased.

Adams spares no one in his description of the fiasco that resulted in the burning of Washington. The Secretary of the Army had made no preparation for the city's defense and later excused himself with the assertion that fortifications would have been too costly. Adams editorializes: "In truth, Armstrong looking at the matter as a military critic decided that the British having no strategic object in capturing Washington, would not make the attempt. Being an indolent man, negligent of detail, he never took unnecessary trouble; and having no proper staff at Washington, he was without military advisers whose opinions he respected."[52] When a general for the defense of the area was finally selected, Madison made his choice on the basis of political acceptability. This worthy, according to Adams, "passed the next month riding between Washington, Baltimore, and points on the lower Potomac and Patuxent, obtaining with great fatigue a personal knowledge of the country. August 1 he established his permanent headquarters at Washington, and the entire result of his labors till that time was the presence of one company of Maryland militia at Bladensburg. No line of defense was selected, no obstructions to the roads were prepared, and not so much as a ditch or a breastwork was marked out or suggested between Annapolis and Washington."[53] When the British landed, they "marched in a leisurely manner through a long-settled country, and met no show of resistance before coming within sight of the Capitol."[54] At long last a feeble force was assembled, but it was utterly routed by the British, who then proceeded to burn the Capitol, the White House and other public buildings. Although much of the ridicule for this state of affairs fell on Madison, Adams felt that it was misplaced. On General Winder he pours all his sarcasm: "When he might have prepared defences, he acted as scout; when he might have fought, he still scouted; when he retreated, he retreated in the wrong direction; when he fought, he thought only of retreat; and whether scouting, retreating, or fighting, he never betrayed an idea."[55] Despite his incompetence, the Secretary of War still supported him in his office. Resentment at the burning of Washington thus fell upon Armstrong, who was forced to resign. James Monroe, who was Secretary of State, then took charge of the War Department as well.

As early as September 1812, Russia offered to mediate between England and the United States, but serious negotiations did not get under way until August 1814. The British sent relatively weak commissioners to Ghent and gave them little discretion. But the Americans sent Albert Gallatin, John Quincy Adams, Henry Clay, and James A. Bayard. By sheer force these men succeeded in wresting from the British a treaty which restored the *status quo ante*, remarkable because of English military superiority. The treaty was signed December 24, 1814. Another of the great ironies of the war was that the great defeat of the British at New Orleans took place after the treaty was signed.

V *America in 1817*

Adams concludes his *History* with four expository chapters: "Economical Results," "Religious and Political Thought," "Literature and Art," and "American Character." In them he takes a much less restricted view of history than the military and political events that occupy most of his nine volumes. The first three of these chapters present an accumulation of facts designed to support the generalizations explained in the last.[56] Adams wishes to prove that an American character does in fact exist, and that he had wanted to study it for the purpose of understanding its part in the movement of history.

The facts that Adams presents show that America had developed in almost every respect since the first inauguration of Thomas Jefferson. The facts about the growth of wealth might seem surprising in view of the economic dislocations of the Napoleonic era. But the high birth rate and consequent increase in population, coupled with the rapid exploitation of resources, made up for the economic waste of warfare. Productivity of the mind, Adams thinks, is even more interesting than that of the economy, and it is easy to prove that the country was generating more sermons, judicial decisions, poems, and essays each succeeding year. All of these facts add up to a justification of the doctrine of progress. Adams sees enough of a line of tendency to project it into the future and thus to justify his optimism.

In his final chapter he concentrates his effort on trying to prove a greater intelligence in the American than in the European.[57] Much of his evidence is drawn from comparisons of American and English handling of the fast-sailing schooner, or the naval cannon, or the musket. Adams's enthusiasm for the accomplishments of the ordinary soldier or sailor by comparison with his officers is entirely acceptable. But his hope that American conditions could evolve a superior person seems naive. Probably he is not expressing so much what had happened between 1817 and 1890 as what he thinks needs to happen after 1890. Teacher that he is, he would be satisfied to induce even a little movement toward a goal that seemed to him as important as the development of intelligence.

VI *Evaluation*

The *History* was well received upon its first publication, though, as Samuels explains, its reception did not satisfy its author, who could have wished for the popular success achieved by Gibbon and Macaulay.[58] It sold moderately well in Adams's lifetime, and it has continued to attract some notice from the academic world. Bradford Perkins says:

No student of these years can fail to owe a great debt to Henry Adams. . . . Adams is almost unreservedly hostile toward the Republican leaders and, as Irving Brant has shown, is not above shading the evidence in a fashion modern historians would consider improper. Although Adams worked more deeply among British manuscripts than any who have followed after him, his attitude toward England is colored with the nationalism of the period in which he wrote. Nevertheless, in the vigor of his judgments, in his capacity for magnificent prose . . . and in the breadth of his vision, Henry Adams still challenges those who follow him.[59]

And John K. Mahon writes: "Henry Adams remains one of our finest historians. About ninety years ago he wrote an operational history of the War of 1812 as a part of his great *History*. . . . This incidental account, in spite of occasional errors and known prejudices, is still the best one on that war." [60] Yvor Winters in *The Anatomy of Nonsense* writes a highly controversial account of Adams's work, but he gives generous credit: "The history is penetrated with precise intelligence in all its parts: it is in this quality, I think, that it surpasses any other historical masterpiece with which I am acquainted. There is greater magnificence in portions of Gibbon, Macaulay, and Motley, but there is seldom the skill of penetration, and there is not the uniformity of success in any of them. And the wit of Adams is invariably the result of understanding instead of the result of its absence."[61]

Other scholars have praised and sometimes blamed Adams on grounds I consider more dubious. Taking his own observations about the possibility of a science of history literally rather than metaphorically, they have interpreted him as a determinist. But this is a logical impossibility, for, as Sir Isaiah Berlin explains,

From the days of Bossuet to those of Hegel and increasingly thereafter, claims have been made, widely varying in degree of generality and confidence, to be able to trace a structure of history (usually *a priori*, for all protests to the contrary), to discover the one and only true pattern into which alone all facts will be found to fit. But this is not, and can never be, accepted by any serious historian who wishes to establish the truth as it is understood by the best critics of his time, working by standards accepted as realistic by his most scrupulous and enlightened fellow workers. For he does not perceive one unique schema as the truth—the only real framework in which alone the facts truly lie; he does not distinguish the one real, cosmic pattern from false ones, as he certainly seeks to distinguish real facts from fiction. The same facts can be arranged in more than one single pattern, seen from several perspectives, displayed in many lights, all of them valid, although some will be more suggestive or fertile in one field than in another, or unify many fields in some illuminating fashion, or, alternatively, bring out disparities and open chasms.[62]

It is precisely in this ability to render history which reflects a multiplicity of viewpoints that the greatness of Henry Adams lies. He was something of the scientist, but he was not only that. He was also all of those contradictory things that made him a man of both the nineteenth and twentieth centuries. Above all, he was not afraid of the inconsistencies he knew he would betray, but he spoke in his own voice, aware that the resonance of the whole man would compensate for the shortcomings he would inevitably reveal.

CHAPTER 8

Tahiti

O N his trip around the world from 1890 to 1892, Adams lingered
four months in Tahiti. Even though he had the companion-
ship of John LaFarge, he soon became bored, as he explained in a
letter to Elizabeth Cameron: "No human being ever saw life more
lovely than here, and I actually sit, hour after hour, doing nothing
but look out at the sky and sea, because it is exquisitely lovely and
makes me so desperately homesick; and I cannot understand either
why it is so beautiful or why it makes me so frantic to escape."[1]
Though he tried his hand at painting and learned from LaFarge to
observe color as he never had before, he did not have enough
artistic talent to keep him interested for long. He saw forbidden
dances performed by "old-gold girls," but his New England fastidi-
ousness made him keep his distance.

But if the physical allurements of the island cloyed, its history did
not. Adams and LaFarge became acquainted with Marau, a chiefess
of the Teva clan, who adopted them into her family.[2] Though it was
something of a joke, as he confessed to Elizabeth Cameron, the
relationship provided him with access to Marau's knowledge of the
island's history. He took notes from her dictation and wrote parts of
a book about Tahiti while on the island, leaving instructions for
Marau to forward other material to him in Washington.[3] After his
return to America he augmented his materials with books published
in Europe and America. He had a volume, *Memoirs of Maura
Taaroa, Last Queen of Tahiti*, privately printed in an edition of ten
copies, copies of which he sent to his Tahitian friends.[4] They
suggested corrections, and he incorporated these in a revised and
expanded book, which he published as *Memoirs of Arii Taimai E.* at
Paris in 1901.

88

I *Arii Taimai's Story*

Although Adams's narrative spans the period from about 1200 to
1850, he chose to write it not as a history but as autobiography. This
form gave him freedom from the imperious demands of history as
research, the need that R. G. Collingwood describes for the historian to formulate answers to questions he has fixed upon be-
forehand.[5] Much of the story of Tahiti was merely legend, an un-
criticized accumulation of details remembered and perhaps embel-
lished from the past. The strongest point of the Tahitian memory of
the past was for genealogy, which had the practical value of enabling
clans to keep out imposters and to insure the rights of those who
belonged. But this manner of delving into the past provided little
material for true history, for it asked few questions about the nature
of man. The method of first-person narration could supply this want
of philosophical depth by stressing the charm of the speaker herself.

This charm arose from giving the old chiefess some of the Adams
irony: she speaks from the standpoint of a representative of a very
old culture in no wise inferior to the European. She becomes a bit of
a Darwinian as she declares that the Tahitian civilization is "better
fitted than any other possible community for the conditions in which
they lived."[6] And she sneers at Rousseau's ideas of the "natural
goodness of the human heart and the moral blessings of a state of
nature,"[7] which had sentimentally been projected onto Tahitian
society by some of its European visitors. She especially inveighs
against the Europeans who wish to be rid of the restraints of their
civilization and who use their own interpretation of Tahitian morality to justify license in themselves. Their incursions help, she
thinks, to break down Tahitian morality. She observes, "The real
code of Tahitian society would have upset the theories of a state of
nature as thoroughly as the guillotine did."[8] Tahitians were not
children, as the European romantics thought, but complex people
functioning in a society which few outsiders bothered to try to understand.

Tahiti before the coming of the European was not peopled by the
likes of Paul and Virginia, but by intense and complex human beings. The earliest legend told by Arii Taimai concerns the beautiful
daughter of Panee, taken away by Hurimaavehi. The angry father
sends insults enough to Hurimaavehi to insure war and then notifies

his own chief, Oro. In the fighting that ensues, Oro traps his enemy
by stealth and carries the battle to such length that his victory is
used to mark the beginning of the Papara clan. Another, much later,
story likewise demonstrates the complexity of the Tahitian personality. Purea, the most important woman of the ruling class of Tahiti,
seeks to elevate her son beyond any other. She erects the great
pyramid at Mahaiatea in his honor, and she requires obeisance far
out of the ordinary for him. Her pride arouses jealousy in others, so
that she eventually finds herself in difficulty despite her great power
and influence. Women like these would not have recognized themselves in the fantasies of Rousseau, but they would have understood
without any difficulty the pride and greed and jealousy at a European court.

Arii Taimai admits that the Tahitians' memory of exact dates
began with June 24, 1767, when Captain Samuel Wallis in H.M.S.
Dolphin arrived at Matavai Bay.[9] Perhaps the impact of the various
European adventurers who stopped at Tahiti made the people
themselves more aware of themselves and of their place in time than
they had been in their primitive state. Certainly the Europeans had
an enormous influence on the lives of the islanders, brief though
their visits seemed. Wallis had been astonished at the numbers of
the people on the island. The second explorer, Captain Cook, in
1767 estimated the combined populations of Tahiti and Moorea at
about two hundred thousand. Contact with Europeans brought
about a disastrous decline in the population of the islands, estimated
at less than twenty thousand in 1797 and five thousand in 1803. The
outsiders were chiefly responsible, because their influence helped
to increase the tensions which led to interisland warfare, and even
more because of the diseases which they brought to a people without immunity.[10]

Captain Cook was not only a very accurate explorer; he also liked
to exert influence on the government of Tahiti itself.[11] He never was
able to understand the system of rank among the Tahitians, and
insisted on regarding one chief as king, after the English fashion.
For Cook this was Tu of Pare, who got his title for the sole reason
that Matavai Bay was the harbor used by the English ships. Iron and
steel were symbols of wealth for the Polynesians, who had not had
these commodities before the arrival of the Europeans. Cook gave
axes and other items to Tu, and this gesture seemed insulting to the
other chiefs. Tu was completely estranged from them when Cook

departed in 1774, and continued so until his return in 1777. Cook tried to assist the man he regarded as king by divine right, and made a proclamation that no one was to attack Tu on pain of Cook's displeasure when he returned. But no Englishman came for eleven years, and in the meantime Tu suffered greatly.

In 1788 H.M.S. *Bounty* arrived with Lt. William Bligh in command. He came "without a doubt that his old acquaintance, Otoo, was King of all Tahiti, and a friend of King George III, to be upheld against every attack, aristocratic or democratic; and what with Cook had been chiefly a matter of convenience and policy became with Bligh a simple matter of course."[12] Tu was in desperate straits, a situation which Bligh tried to remedy. Arii Taimai comments sarcastically:

If Tu's situation had not been tragical to the island, it would have been comical. As long as British ships were in Matavai Bay, he was rich and powerful; his house was filled with all that made wealth: axes, fish-hooks, cloth, nails, beads; and cattle, goats, or whatever the ships contained. No other chief received gifts except in trifling amounts. The instant the British ships disappeared, this wealth became an irresistible temptation to Tu's neighbors and a fatal danger to himself. Tu had been a sort of milch-cow to the chiefs of Eimeo, Faaa, and Hitiaa. He begged the gifts which they were to squeeze from him.[13]

Bligh left Tu arms, which were augmented when sixteen mutineers from the *Bounty* returned to place themselves under Tu's protection.[14] They helped him to establish his ascendancy over the other chiefs, a condition which prevailed even after their capture by Captain Edwards of the *Pandora*. It was about this time that Tu took the name Pomare (night-cough) to distinguish himself from his young son, also named Tu, who was given to night coughs. He did not give up his official name; he was merely following the custom of the Tahitian chiefs, who often had several nicknames. But this one stuck, and the name Pomare would continue to the end of the dynasty at the abdication of King Pomare V in 1880.

The European governments had lost interest in Tahiti by the end of the eighteenth century, and there ensued a long period in which records were very poorly kept. It was a period of great bloodshed, in which flourished "the worst and most bloodthirsty of all—Tu, the first Christian king."[15] He was the son of the first Tu, and he later also took the name of Pomare. This was a period in which the missionaries were active, sometimes as much, ironically, in bloody warfare as in the saving of souls. They did not hesitate to ask for muskets for Tu, "in order to preserve peace."[16] When they heard of an impending battle, they wrote, "We rejoice that the Lord of Hosts is the God of the heathen as well as the Captain of the armies of Israel; and while the potsherds of the earth are dashing themselves to pieces one against the other, they are but fulfilling his determinate counsels and foreknowledge."[17] Arii Taimai explains: "This Calvinistic or fatalistic view of the heathen justified or excused every possible action on all sides of every question."[18] Their tolerance for Tu's cruelty helped them to establish control over the islands, which they maintained for forty years.

The rule of the missionaries was broken by the failure of the British to support them sufficiently after the French had moved to support their own Catholic missionaries.[19] The chiefs, feeling themselves without protection under missionary rule, petitioned the French to intervene. In the negotiations for this transfer, Arii Taimai had a leading part. She went as a leader of great importance to convince Queen Pomare to accept French hegemony in return for a guarantee that she would retain her title and position in the country. The queen was undecided for months, but at last realizing that the British would not help her, she assented. Arii Taimai, by refusing to accept the offer of the crown for herself, had helped to secure the peace of the country, for which she received the thanks of the French governor, Bruat.

II *Evaluation*

The *Memoirs of Arii Taimai E.* is the least known of Adams's books and it is likely to remain so, for its intricate tracing of Tahitian genealogies soon tires the reader unaccustomed to Polynesian names. Literary scholars have called the book a failure and a bore, or have seen it as an exercise which anticipates *Mont-Saint-Michel and Chartres*. But Adams's book seems to have retained some value for the specialist historian and anthropologist. In a recent three-volume work entitled *Ancient Tahitian Society*, Douglas L. Oliver cites Adams again and again.[20] In a few instances he points out errors, but more often he seems to rely on him as an authority.

Despite the strange technique and subject matter of the *Memoirs*, the book shows many of the strengths of Adams the historian. Above all he is the ironist who uses his barbs to put down those who deny others their full humanity. For him the meaning of Tahitian history says much about the cruelty of man to man, but especially the cruelty of the privileged Europeans to the disadvantaged Tahitians. And yet through the whole narrative runs a note of optimism in the voice of Arii Taimai herself. If humanity could produce someone as rational as she, perhaps it might be worth saving after all.

CHAPTER 9

Mont-Saint-Michel and Chartres

IN the summer of 1895, while on a tour of western France with Henry Cabot Lodge and his family, Adams wrote to Elizabeth Cameron: "And so to Chartres where we passed two hours yesterday afternoon, and after thirty-five years of postponed intentions, I worshipped at last before the splendor of the great glass Gods. Chartres is a beautiful gate by which to leave the Norman paradise, as Amiens is a beautiful gate to enter."[1] Obviously, some of the enthusiasm that would animate *Mont-Saint-Michel and Chartres* was already stirring, perhaps had been stirring for those thirty-seven years since he first encountered the medieval part of Antwerp.[2] Those years of teaching medieval history at Harvard, when sometimes he found himself forced to examine as many as four books for his classes the next day, gave him a strong general background. More recently, the instruction he had taken from John LaFarge on his trip to Japan and on another to Tahiti had taught him to distinguish subtleties of color,[3] and LaFarge had also taught him that Chartres had the best stained glass in the world.[4] Another influence was John Ruskin, whose studies of Gothic architecture had insisted on the contrast between the medieval and the modern spirit, between an age of faith and one of unbelief.[5]

But Adams was not one to rush into print with his first inspiration. Each summer as he returned to Paris for his customary stay of several months, he would travel all over northern France in search of twelfth-century churches for study. He spent countless hours examining stone and glass at Le Mans, Caen, Coutances, St. Lô, Mont-Saint-Michel, and numerous other churches.[6] He read voraciously, especially in students of Romanesque and Gothic architecture. But he was not attempting so much to accumulate a large number of facts about the Middle Ages as to learn to feel the spirit of the twelfth century. His success in capturing that spirit makes

Mont-Saint-Michel and Chartres the best book of the medieval revival in America. But it was not Adams's adherence to the ideas of a group that made his book important; it was his ability to dramatize an interesting mind operating in an interesting context.

I *Point of View*

In almost all of his work Adams had relied on an Olympian pose as a device for giving ease to his reader: like Gibbon he commented with assurance from a vast accumulation of material, and his reader could only follow meekly, happy that he had so sure a guide. But in writing the *Memoirs of Arii Taimai E.* he found that his documents were too scanty to allow him to feel secure. So he made a virtue of necessity by creating a persona whose interpretation became the center of interest in the narrative. The fact that a non-Western woman would dare to offer comments about Christian missionaries, or British explorers, or even her own people gave special flavor to the history of Tahiti. Unfortunately, this experiment concerned subject matter too exotic for ready assimilation by Westerners, and Adams's book achieved only a small readership.

When Adams decided to write a book on the Middle Ages, he could have chosen to be Olympian, had he so wished. True, he was aware of the dangers of the pose, as he had admitted in his essay "Count Edward de Crillion," but he had covered for himself by claiming the right to a certain margin of error. His problem in *Chartres* was to avoid the weight of pedantry: he wanted to present the feeling of the Middle Ages. He knew that much of what he wanted to communicate would have been known to the rudest peasant of the twelfth century, though he also knew that a twentieth-century farmer might find the peasant's feeling incomprehensible without explanation. But if one were to have the feeling, he would have to minimize somehow the explanation; all too often facts turn dry.

To solve this problem, Adams creates another persona, a witty and learned old uncle who has removed himself from the responsibilities of the lecture hall by posing as a summer tourist. He confesses to some of the limitations of his New England, Calvinistic outlook, but he shows at the same time some of the ease of the well-to-do gentleman. Adams creates for him another persona, a niece who never speaks, but whose presence stimulates the uncle's voice. Intelligent but uninitiated in the mysteries of the medieval

world, she limits what the uncle can say and at the same time gives
him his opportunity. Though he cannot present the technicalities of
scholarship, he can bring to her attention the objects which will
enable her to feel the life of the middle ages.

Chartres would not have succeeded so well if it were not for the
highly symbolic nature of the material under examination. The
uncle shows himself especially sensitive to what Susanne K. Langer
calls the "presentational symbol," that which evokes meaning without having to employ the discursive symbolism of language.[7]
Chartres is full of confrontations with presentational symbols—por-
tals, spires, windows, to name only a few. Adams means for them to
be interpreted with something like the integration of sensibility and
intellect in the formula that later became so important to T. S. Eliot
and his followers. The niece seems to represent the sensibility; the
uncle, the intellect. His part may seem to be the more important
because he has to give the book continuity, but he must accommodate himself to her need for feeling. The effect of Adams's control of
point of view is to reassure the reader that the persona will indeed
allow him to feel with accuracy the symbols of the medieval world.

II   *Romanesque and Gothic*

In his very first sentence, the uncle directs the niece's eye upward from the strand as he also directs her mind toward an emotion
which the uncle describes as "the deepest man ever felt,—the
struggle of his own littleness to grasp the infinite."[8] To do so, man
needs to overcome the limitation of his finite nature, and this, the
uncle implies, he can do by the use of symbols. His actual words,
"The Archangel loved heights,"[9] emphasize, by a device which he
would use again and again, the anthropomorphic aspect of St.
Michael while putting him in a context nearly supernatural. This
juxtaposition is a device to help the uninitiated niece to feel the
angel's symbolic force. She can use her own sense of vertigo to feel
him on his mount, the place associating him with heaven and symbolizing the energetic or masculine principle. That he is implanted
beside the sea, symbolizing the creative or feminine principle,
makes him the more impressive. She might remember that he is the
angel who spoke to Moses on Mount Sinai (Acts 7:38) and is, as the
uncle puts it, "nearest to God." He is the guardian of the Church,
the slayer of the dragon in the war in heaven (Revelation 12:7).

Lest he leave a wrong impression, the uncle moves quickly into the church itself to demonstrate the danger even for a man of God in the Middle Ages of reaching toward the infinite. Abbot Hildebert in building his nave had the opportunity of making his church secure by removing enough rock from the summit of the mount to give him a flat surface.[10] But to do so would have cost him thirty feet in the height of his church. He built as high as possible, though this posture required him to use masonry for the foundation of most of his building. The part supported by solid rock remained secure, but the nave began to fall as early as 1300, and three of his seven arches had been pulled down by 1776. Even a man of God, apparently obeying the command of the Archangel Michael, could be trapped by pride.

But the uncle's lessons sometimes contain ambiguities, such as those which appear in the story of Abbot Hildebert's choir.[11] It, too, began to fall because of its inadequate foundation, but unlike the nave it was rebuilt. For the new part the architect chose, not the original Romanesque style of 1058, but the current late Gothic of 1521. He achieved a perfect harmony of styles because, as the uncle puts it, the masculine of the Romanesque was married to the feminine of the Gothic, a process which the uncle describes: "The simple serious silent dignity and energy of the eleventh century have gone. Something more complicated stands in their place; graceful, self-conscious, rhetorical, and beautiful as perfect rhetoric, with its clearness, light, and line, and the wealth of tracery that verges on the florid."[12] In other words, the symbolic content of each style makes it sufficient unto itself, so that no conflict need arise in the transition from one to the other. In this instance the problem of the direction of movement in history seems to be resolved by the ability of the symbol to assimilate and to reconcile disparate elements in its milieu.

The uncle finds a second problem of transition in the cathedral at Mantes,[13] which incorporates Romanesque elements into an early Gothic design. The architect solved some of the problem of fenestration by resorting to a series of small, round windows, each set in its own small tunnel, a device which obviously recalls the round arch of the Romanesque. He also used one of the earliest rose windows, and in this setting the repetition and enlargement of shape demonstrates very well the debt of the Gothic church-builders to the Romanesque. The symbolic shape of the rose window and its ability to satisfy the greed for light of the Gothic builders made it an inescapable choice, but it fitted inconveniently in the pointed arch. Mantes affords yet another lesson in transition: it was built on almost the same plan as Notre Dame de Paris. When the latter was torn down, it was rebuilt in a design which eliminated many of the transitional elements of the original. Mantes serves, then, not only to remind the viewer of the ability of the symbol to effect a transition from the problems of one age to those of another; it also points toward the triumph of the Gothic over the Romanesque.

III *Chartres*

Despite the title of the book, even Mont-Saint-Michel is only preliminary: Chartres itself is the primary object of the uncle's pilgrimage. Despite the enormous possibilities in the ten thousand figures carved on the outside of the cathedral, he chooses not to begin with a survey of them, as some of his critics have thought would have been best. Instead, he takes an approach like that he used at Mont-Saint-Michel: he first directs the niece's eyes upward to the spires.[14] Although St. Bernard had thought the flèche an unnecessary, perhaps even harmful, part of the church, the uncle knows that the American niece needs to have her mind directed away from the mundane. The spires of Chartres offer much room for instruction, for the niece, more likely than not, will prefer the new tower to the old. The uncle explains that the simplicity of the old spire makes it one of the finest pieces of architecture in existence, a perfect rendering of the emotions of the age of the Second Crusade. And he calls on Viollet-le-Duc, the famous architect, as authority for his admiration of the proportions of the tower and of the transition from the square base on which it rests to the octagon of the tower itself. But he has no such admiration for the new tower. Although it is four hundred years younger than the old, in spirit it is four hundred years older, more suited for the Dark Ages than for an age which built St. Peter's. The uncle cannot bring himself to see any possibility of reconciling the two approaches, and he concludes with an irony that smacks of John Ruskin: "Yet it may be beautiful still; the poets derided the wrinkles of Diane de Poitiers at the very moment when King Henry II idealized her with the homage of a Don Quixote; an atmosphere of physical beauty and decay hangs about the whole Renaissance."[15]

The essential symbolism At Chartres, the uncle contends, is feminine. To the tourist this fact is announced by the north portal of the cathedral, which is devoted to Mary. In the center of the portal there is a scene depicting the crowning of Mary as Queen of Heaven. And the other figures on the portal—all seven hundred of them—are designed to reinforce this interpretation of Mary as a source of power. The uncle is emphatic: "Unless we feel this assertion of the divine right in the Queen of Heaven, apart from the Trinity, yet one with it, Chartres is unintelligible."[16] Even in the carving on the south portal, devoted to the Son, the interpretation of Mary as queen is grudgingly accepted. Most of the carvings on this door are entirely masculine, but high above the door are two representations of Mary crowned.

At this point the uncle speaks of Mary as an earthly queen, commanding her subjects to prepare her cathedral in a manner suitable to her dignity. He does not intend any disrespect to her; he is only trying to convince the niece of the feeling of those who built the cathedral. He says: "If you are to get the full enjoyment of Chartres, you must, for the time, believe in Mary as Bernard and Adam did, and feel her presence as the architects did, in every stone they placed, and every touch they chiselled."[17] Because they felt her presence so keenly, they labored hard to find a style which would fit her requirements of "space, light, convenience; and colour decoration to harmonize the whole."[18] Again, the uncle's device of attributing personality to the Virgin sometimes seems whimsical to the point of irreverence, but he is trying to shake the protestant niece out of her stiff idealization of the Virgin, an attitude that makes her emotionally inaccessible. To the Middle Ages her symbolism had expressed something far more complex than the New England girl would understand; Calvinism may have been as logical as the schools, but it taught little about love or hate or mercy.

In the stained glass of Chartres the uncle finds God's plenty. Amusingly, his New England reticence surfaces, so that he confesses that he is "ashamed to be as extravagant as one wants to be."[19] Apologizing for having to reason about something that needs only to be felt, he consoles himself with the pedagogue's excuse that "perhaps not one in a thousand of the English-speaking race—does feel it, or can feel it even when explained to him, for we have lost many senses."[20] Undaunted, he takes the niece straight to the oldest and best glass in the cathedral, that of the three lancet windows above the Royal Portal. In the opinion of Viollet-le-Duc, he says, the Tree of Jesse window is the finest stained glass ever made. Its superiority derives in part from the artist's handling of the color blue, which is the equivalent of light in the complex color symbolism of glass. The uncle elaborates:

If the Tree of Jesse window teaches anything at all, it is that the artist thought first of controlling his light, but he wanted to do it not in order to dim the colours; on the contrary he toiled, like a jeweller setting diamonds and rubies, to increase their splendour. If his use of blue teaches this lesson, his use of green proves it. The outside border of the Tree of Jesse is a sort of sample which our schoolmaster Viollet-le-Duc sets, from which he requires us to study out the scheme, beginning with the treatment of light, and ending with the value of the emerald green ground in the corners.[21]

For all his admiration of this individual window, the uncle does not forget that it exists to glorify the Virgin. Again he directs the niece's eye, this time to the central window in the group of three: "Look at the central window! Naturally, there sits the Virgin, with her genealogical tree on her left, and her Son's testimony on her right, to prove her double divinity."[22] And, referring to the windows of the group as a whole, he declares emphatically:

All are marked by the hand of the Chartres Virgin. They are executed not merely for her, but by her. At Saint-Denis the Abbé Suger appeared,—it is true that he was prostrate at her feet, but still he appeared. At Chartres no one—no suggestion of a human agency—was allowed to appear; the Virgin permitted no one to approach her, even to adore. She is enthroned above, as Queen and Empress and Mother, with the symbols of exclusive and universal power. Below her, she permitted the world to see the glories of her earthly life;—the Annunciation, Visitation, and Nativity; the Magi; King Herod; the Journey to Egypt; and the single medallion, which shows the gods of Egypt falling from their pedestals at her coming, is more entertaining than a whole picture-gallery of oil paintings.[23]

And so the uncle goes around the cathedral surveying the windows, telling stories of their origins and symbolism, and always insisting that the niece appreciate the personality of the Virgin as reflected in her choices of symbolism for her glory. One of the most interesting windows for the uncle is that of the Prodigal Son. Originally, the uncle points out, the story had been interpreted as God's favoring the elder son, or the Jews, with divine law, while he gave the younger, or the Gentiles, the law of nature. The younger squandered his inheritance on Aristotle, but the two sons were reconciled when Christ was sacrificed as a symbol of reunion. This version of the story had gone out of fashion about the time the Chartres Prodigal window was executed; its version of the story is the more familiar one. But the Virgin did not grant this window the place of honor it found in many other cathedrals. The uncle puzzles over her decision:

> She was rather fond of prodigals, and gentle toward the ladies who consumed the prodigal's substance. She admitted Mary Magdalen and Mary the Gipsy to her society. She fretted little about Aristotle so long as the prodigal adored her, and naturally the prodigal adored her almost to the exclusion of the Trinity. She always cared less for her dignity than was to be wished. Especially in the nave and on the porch, among the peasants, she liked to appear as one of themselves; she insisted on lying in bed, in a stable, with the cows and asses about her, and her baby in a cradle by the bedside, as though she had suffered like other women, though the Church insisted she had not.[24]

The uncle's stress on the universality of the symbolism of Mary doubtless seems strange to a New England niece, who might have thought herself one of the elect. But it is no more strange than Gauguin's *Ia Orana Maria*, which transports the Virgin and the Christ Child to Polynesia.[25] Perhaps Gauguin and Adams both derived some of their inspiration from Tahiti, where by only four days they missed meeting in June 1891.[26] At any rate, both men seemed more willing to stress the Christian doctrine of love than had Adams's Calvinist ancestors.

IV Women

The idealization of the Virgin at Chartres leads the uncle to a favorite theme—the superiority of women. In the Middle Ages, he says, this "was not a fancy, but a fact."[27] For proof, his primary example is Eleanor of Guienne, "the greatest of all French-women."[28] As a queen, her most admirable quality was her inability to accept defeat. When she was married to Louis VII of France, she was a popular and effective ruler. The uncle interprets her decline from power in France as the doing of Bernard of Clairvaux, a man even more powerful than she. Her infidelities to Louis while she was in Palestine on the Second Crusade caused the annulment of her marriage, but the uncle doubts the substance of the accusation. True, she married Henry of Anjou only two months later. And when he succeeded to the English throne, she became Queen of England, a title she retained for fifty years.

More important, in the uncle's view, was the part Eleanor played with her daughter Mary of Champagne in the school of "courteous love." As the Virgin used the power of spiritual love to improve the people, Eleanor used earthly love to improve life at court. For the uncle the most important contribution of this school is its ability to dramatize life so that it became bearable in spite of its defects. The uncle explains: "Life had miseries enough, but few shadows deeper than those of the imaginative lover, or the terrors of ghosts at night. Men's imaginative lover, or the terrors of ghosts at night. Men's imaginations ran riot, but did not keep them awake."[29] The psychological need in man for some "illusion," for some center about which his imagination can turn, seems as deeply fixed in the uncle's mind as it was in that of Axel Heyst in Conrad's *Victory*.[30] Stories such as those of Tristram or Aucassins might have caused Don Quixote to depart completely from reality, but that was his fault. For most men the "illusions" are more important than ordinary reality. The uncle concludes that it is a matter of interpretation: "Illusion for illusion, courteous love, in Thibaut's hands, or in the hands of Dante and Petrarch, was as substantial as any other convention;—the balance of trade, the rights of man, or the Athanasian Creed. In that sense the illusions alone were real; if the Middle Ages had reflected only what was practical, nothing would have survived for us."[31]

The convention of "courteous love" furnishes the uncle with illustrations of this principle. The story of Aucassins and Nicolette focuses everything through the medium of love: the hero has fallen in love with his father's god-daughter, who has been brought up in his family. Aucassins wants to marry Nicolette, but his father wants him to make a marriage with a woman of high station. The father promises Nicolette to Aucassins in exchange for service in battle, but reneges, and Aucassins is imprisoned for his failure to slaughter the enemy. Eventually he escapes and finds Nicolette, who has escaped and is living in a little hut in the forest. She binds up his wounds and they ride away, caring naught for anything but love. This story and that of Robin and Marion make woman "always the stronger force";[32] she is always "the practical guide; the one who keeps her head, even in love."[33] The uncle approves in his Victorian manner:

Like all the romans, or nearly all, "Aucassins" is singularly pure and refined. Apparently the ladies of courteous love frowned on coarseness and allowed no licence. Their power must have been great, for the best romans are as free from grossness as the "Chanson de Roland" itself, or the church glass, or the illuminations in the manuscripts; and as long as the power of the Church ruled good society, this decency continued. As far as women were concerned, they seem always to have been more clean than the men, except when men painted them in colours which men liked best.[34]

Perhaps the uncle's own illusion shows here more clearly than in the other parts of his book, but he is not likely to allow his monologue to be interrupted by a New England niece.

V *The Decline of Unity into Rationality*

In his interpretation of the High Middle Ages as a period of unity, the uncle contrasts it by inference with the multiplicity of his own time. After showing the splendors brought about in that golden age, he introduces in his last chapters material to show how the decline of unity and the onset of multiplicity came about. He implies that the causes involved the kind of thinking fostered within the Church itself. Instead of being content with the symbols which it had in such abundance, it sought to have Reason as well.

The uncle introduces the niece to churchly disputations in the story of Abélard. The love affair with Héloise receives little attention in the uncle's narration; none of its passion or violence is allowed to show. Instead, Abélard is placed in the center of the stage in his capacity as disputant.[35] First, he debates with William of Champeaux, the realist, whose philosophical position would seem close to that which had produced the unity of Chartres. Abélard took the nominalist side and won his disputation by forcing William to recognize the tendency of realism to shade over into pantheism. But, as the uncle points out, Abélard's nominalism offered no protection, even though it was adopted by the Church. His conceptualism was totally unsatisfactory:

Unity either is, or is not. If soldiers, no matter in what number, can never make an army, and worshippers, though in millions, do not make a Church, and all humanity united would not necessarily constitute a State, equally little can their concepts, individual or united, constitute the one or the other. Army, Church, and State, each is an organic whole, complex beyond all possible addition of units, and not a concept at all, but rather an animal that thinks, creates, devours, and destroys. The attempt to bridge the chasm between multiplicity and unity is the oldest problem of philosophy, religion and science, but the flimsiest bridge of all is the human concept, unless somewhere, within or beyond it, an energy not individual is hidden; and in that case the old question instantly reappears: What is that energy?[36]

The uncle's comments on Abélard's later disputations about the Holy Ghost serve to amplify the position he has already taken. In a long digression he points out that "the Trinity was intended to explain the eternal and primary problem of the process by which unity could produce diversity."[37] The Church had been compelled to take the duality of Father and Son, but philosophy required a third element. This solution introduced far more complexity than might have seemed the case: "In philosophy, the product of two units was not a third unit, but diversity, multiplicity, infinity."[38] Yet Abélard did not accept the yearning of simple people for the identification of the Holy Ghost with the Virgin Mary; he sought by dialectic to remove the mystery which cloaked that part of the Trinity. For long the Church was tolerant, but eventually he aroused the opposition of Bernard. The uncle obviously sympathizes with the latter: "For several thousand years mankind has stared Infinity in the face without pretending to be the wiser; the pretension of Abélard was that, by his dialectic method, he could explain the Infinite, while all other theologists talked mere words."[39] And in his commitment to logic, he ended by making God a logician, totally bound by necessity. This Bernard could not accept.

The uncle gives over his final chapter to St. Thomas Aquinas, whose work he wishes to study as art, though, like Beauvais Cathedral, it perhaps overreached itself.[40] The uncle explains that God is the Prime Motor who supplies all creatures in the universe with energy. In the creation He did not act by succession; He willed everything into being and at the same time willed that it should develop in time. Some events he willed would be bound by necessity; others were contingent. Man's freedom of choice falls into the latter category: in the creation he was given mind, which enabled him to choose. Yet man was not left completely unsupported in the creation: through the operation of Grace he could receive sufficient energy from God to help him to carry out the divine purpose.

Although the uncle admires "the power of broad and lofty generalization" that enabled St. Thomas to construct so strong and yet so simple an edifice, he offers several objections to his reasoning. He cites with some sympathy the charges of his critics that "he has reduced God to a mechanism and man to a passive conductor of force."[41] He notes with surprise St. Thomas's "astonishingly scientific method." Both St. Thomas and the scientist aim at the resolution of the problem of multiplicity and unity. Science has the difficulty of starting with multiplicity. In one direction of development it can find unity at the extreme of infinite complexity; at the other end it posits another kind of unity. The uncle does not name the concept of entropy at this point, but he is obviously thinking of a scientific universe every bit as inhuman as was that set moving by St. Thomas's Prime Motor.

One of the uncle's most ironical commentaries on the system of Thomism is his comparison of the natures of God and of man: "Strange as it sounds, although man thought himself hardly treated in respect to freedom, yet, if freedom meant superiority, man was in action much the superior of God, Whose freedom suffered, from Saint Thomas, under restraints that man never would have tolerated."[42] Man could refuse to act or could commit suicide; God could do neither. Man could sin incessantly; God was confined to absolute goodness. Man could be absurd; God could not. Obviously, the uncle is being playful about the attributes of God dependent upon His perfection. But his wit has its serious side, too. St. Thomas's system provided unity, which the uncle's mind craves. At the same time it was forced into placing such limits on God as to reveal that St. Thomas, too, had failed to solve the problem of multiplicity. He had imagined a God who could satisfy the medieval need for logic, but it was obvious that he never could have imagined twentieth-century complexity.

The uncle closes *Mont-Saint-Michel and Chartres* with a paean to the idea of unity.[43] The architects of the Gothic cathedrals sought to express in their buildings the idea of unity as found in the institution of the Church. They succeeded admirably, but their success could not be continued, because the idea of unity itself became more difficult to sustain. The uncle does not justify the increased complexity of the modern world by the doctrine of progress; he attributes the movement from unity to multiplicity to changed conditions which exhibit another aspect of the world. The awareness of the possibility of change, he suggests, may have been the quality that made the Gothic cathedrals the most expressive examples of

architecture ever erected. For the uncle the flying buttress sym-
bolizes the whole range of emotions—the fears and the aspirations—of all those for whom the churches were a means of expression. In the final analysis, then, the unity achieved at Chartres came
by force of the symbol that brought together both idea and feeling.

VI *Evaluation*

Yvor Winters in *The Anatomy of Nonsense* offers one of the
harshest critiques of the ideas of *Chartres* and the *Education* that
has yet been published. Reading Adams quite literally, and gener-
ously projecting some of the ideas that would-be positivist scholars
imagine they see in Adams, he declares: "Like a true Calvinist and a
true determinist, he turned at once, for his answer to the Nature of
the Universe, and sought to show that the whole universe, as a
single mechanism, was running down."[44] If this is the case, then
that which was earlier in time had to be better, and Adams twists his
facts to suit the case: "Adams' view of the Middle Ages, which has
been adopted by Eliot and his followers, is merely a version of the
Romantic Golden Age; the thirteenth century as they see it never
existed, and their conviction that major intellectual and spiritual
achievement is possible only in such a Utopia can do nothing but
paralyze human effort."[45] Winters's interpretation is only an extreme example of the kind of unfavorable criticism *Chartres* has
attracted from time to time. Adams has been found guilty of getting
some of the facts of his history wrong, and he has been accused of
failure to understand some of the Catholic doctrines. Certainly if
Adams were as weak in facing the realities of scholarship or the
harshness of modern life as he has been painted, he would deserve
severe criticism.

These strictures against *Chartres* come from a literal mindedness
that ignores the work itself. Point of view is everything in a book like
Chartres: Adams creates the uncle, and attributes every word in the
book to him as a dramatic monologue addressed to a niece who
never speaks. The uncle does seem to be tinged with New England,
but it would be hard to call him a Calvinist, as indeed it would be
impossible to make Adams himself a Calvinist. The uncle is certainly
not a determinist and neither was Adams himself; both are far too
interested in the symbol to make determinism easy. The uncle is not
trying to expound Catholic doctrine or to make a convert of the

niece. Nor did Henry Adams ever seem interested in such explanations, for he was not writing a polemical book.

After nearly three quarters of a century, *Mont-Saint-Michel and Chartres* retains all of its power to evoke the spirit of the Middle Ages. More than any other book, it captures the feeling of the Age of Faith. Adams's persona examines one by one the symbols of that age and allows his imagination to play over their meaning for both past and present. By this process he concentrates and focuses the energy of each symbol so that the reader feels its power. The speaker unblushingly omits much that belonged to the life of the Middle Ages, but he does so in order to stress the part of medieval experience most relevant to succeeding generations. Adams's method of presentation satisfies almost perfectly the need expressed in T. S. Eliot's "Tradition and the Individual Talent" for feeling the presence of the past in the present. Adams's ability to bring the past to life by allowing it to share in the life of the present makes *Mont-Saint-Michel and Chartres* a literary masterpiece.

CHAPTER 10

The Education of Henry Adams

A S the historian in Henry Adams knew, he studied the cathedrals of France at least partly to discover himself and his age. No one could possibly go back to the thirteenth century except in imagination, and the journey always involves a comparison of past and present. He found in the earlier age what he described as unity, though others have failed to see the thirteenth century as anything but a troubled time of contradictory tendencies. His own age he began to describe as "multiplicity." Because he had already set the thirteenth century at the opposite pole from the twentieth, it was only natural that he should write a sequel to his thirteenth-century book as one set in the twentieth.

It is important to remember that Adams did not claim that the thirteenth century was totally unified, or even that the unity achieved in Thomistic philosophy was satisfactory. What the thirteenth century did achieve was a unified and therefore convincing symbolism. It had these qualities because it found, for example, in the flying buttress of the famous last paragraph of *Mont-Saint-Michel and Chartres* an objective correlative of a whole complex of feeling and thought common to men of that age. It was expression at its highest reach, and Henry Adams had had the habit of writing too long not to know how hard, yet how important, was some form of ultimate expression.

So his *Education* was a quest, as Ernest Samuels has said,[1] but it was a quest for a philosophy unified enough to support a set of symbols. Many people have worried about Adams's lack of knowledge of Thomism and his egregious errors in the discussion of science. Still, Adams knew that, however refined, no system of theology or of science can be perfect. The theologian or scientist abreast of his field will know its points of vulnerability and the steps to be taken to allow for its defects. The important thing about a system for a man of letters is that it be suggestive enough—that it generate symbols that will contain enough to appeal to men's imaginations. The Church, whatever the defects of reasoning in Abélard or Aquinas, had certainly appealed to the imagination. The problem for Adams was whether or not science and multiplicity could do the same. Adams was well aware of the problem of perspective; eight hundred years had made it certain that the symbolism of Chartres would continue to appeal. But a twentieth-century man seeking to know as much about his own age must necessarily be less certain.

In stepping back to tell his own life in the third person, Adams returned to the Olympian perspective that he had used for satirical purposes from the beginning of his writing career. If he had paraded his bleeding heart through all the failures he described, he would have made himself a complete sentimentalist. As it is, he emerges a "manikin" Lilliputian in scale, and therefore petty and somewhat ludicrous. Ironically, he made his mask all too well for some of his readers; even so capable a critic as Yvor Winters can take all too seriously what Adams intended to be funny.

I *Childhood*

The manikin born in Boston, on February 16, 1838, came into a world that was extraordinarily well provided with the symbols of American history. The Massachusetts State House, Boston, Quincy, the Adams family itself—no one was better supplied than he. Most important of all, he was born into a family whose members had long ago learned how to use their minds. Adams makes very clear the development of the mind of the child in the contrast he learned to make between Boston and Quincy: "Town was restraint, law, unity. Country, only seven miles away, was liberty, diversity, outlawry, the endless delight of mere sense impressions given by nature for nothing, and breathed by boys without knowing it."[2] Quincy held even more important symbols: the old house and its content of mementos of the many diplomatic voyages of the Adamses. More important, John Quincy Adams still lived there in the boy's youth; his bald head in church impressed his grandson's imagination with its ability to suggest what the old man had meant to his country. For education the most important event of his childhood was the time that old John Quincy Adams put on his hat, took his rebellious grandson by the hand, and walked with him in silence on a hot

summer morning to school.[3] Few grandfathers could have given
more symbolic force to the beginnings of a quest for education.

The grandfather did not succeed in making the boy like the formalities of school: the discipline of memorizing he found irksome.
Yet the four studies that he thought he should have mastered all
required the application of the memory: mathematics, French,
German, and Spanish. One visit to Washington at the age of twelve
seemed worth more for education than all the time he spent in
school.[4] He saw for the first time the slovenliness associated with
the slave system, and he associated the bad Virginia roads with the
wickedness of slavery. Strangely in contrast with everything in this
setting stood Mount Vernon, like Quincy a remnant of the
eighteenth century. Of Washington the man, Adams says that he
was the one figure in American history whose image he did not have
to adjust as education proceeded. Symbolically, Washington was
always adequate.

Adams becomes ironical as he considers Harvard College, symbolically associated with Massachusetts from the earliest days of the
colony and with the Adams family since John Adams. He says that
no one took Harvard seriously. Ernest Samuels goes to great length
to refute Adams's charges,[5] demonstrating that he was indeed exposed to a great deal of subject matter. But Samuels is giving a
defense of the academic establishment, while Adams is describing
the lack of imagination in teaching, what Whitehead calls "inert
ideas." Adams withholds praise from all but two of his teachers.
Louis Agassiz stimulated his imagination, he says, with his lectures
about the Glacial Period and paleontology. And James Russell Lowell introduced from Germany the practice of allowing students to
read with him in his study. The effects of their imaginations remained with Adams long after he had outgrown their ideas. Yet he
thought that the work he did in four years at Harvard could easily
have been done in four months of later life. And he concludes his
chapter on Harvard, "Education had not begun."[6]

II *Antiheroes*

In youth and early manhood Adams found a number of persons to
whom he gave heroic status. Chief among these was John Quincy
Adams, followed closely by George Washington, John Adams, Edward Gibbon, Charles Francis Adams, James Russell Lowell, and
Louis Agassiz. Perhaps some of his feeling was youthful idealization,

for he wrote very little unfavorable to any of these men. What they had in common was a wide perspective; none of them could be called parochial in his interests. Most of them were persons of action who had solid accomplishments to their credit. Most had great self-discipline. Adams's heroes did not include a great religious leader, or a musician, or a man of business. If his heroes are an indication of his set of values, Adams seems almost completely conventional in his acceptance of New England attitudes.

As he began to move onto a larger stage than his native Massachusetts, he acquired few new heroes. Instead, he encountered many who seemed the antithesis of his early idols. In his tour as private secretary to his father, the ambassador to England, he met many who aroused his suspicions. The English had shown far more sympathy for the Confederacy than Adams could stomach, because he regarded the Southerner as a mindless, indolent person given to the wickedness of slavery. A part of Adams's education was to be a study of the types of Englishmen who would engage in support of the slave power. Adams opines: "The most costly tutors in the world were provided for him at public expense—Lord Palmerston, Lord Russell, Lord Westbury, Lord Selborne, Mr. Gladstone, Lord Granville, and their associates, paid by the British Government; William H. Seward, Charles Francis Adams, William Maxwell Evarts, Thurlow Weed, and other considerable professors employed by the American government; but there was only one student to profit by this immense staff of teachers. The private secretary alone sought education."[7] The problem the young man gave himself in this school was whether or not human nature in politics could be trusted. He felt that the English leaders offered good subjects for study because "all of these gentlemen were superlatively honorable." Obviously he intends an irony here, for as he watched he felt sure of a conspiracy. Lord Russell, he thought, had from the very beginning planned to recognize the Confederacy in order to break up the Union. He watched Palmerston with suspicion, and only long after the events did he find out enough to realize that he had judged him wrongly. Nearly forty years later, he read in Gladstone's diary the entries that caused him to feel that he had been the only true and effective supporter of Jefferson Davis in the group. What these events contributed to education seemed simple: perhaps the only surprising thing about them is that Adams should have been surprised so late at human duplicity.

Marian Hooper's letter of May 28, 1865, to Mary Louise Shaw, written long before her marriage to Henry Adams, conveys the tone of superpatriotism that surged through the North at the conclusion of the Civil War.[8] The country had felt the war, and it likewise felt a sense of relief at its end. It also felt a sense of accomplishment, and it wished to honor its heroes. Despite the pictures of Matthew Brady, which showed the grimly realistic side of war, there was still a tendency to idealize war, and particularly the role of the hero. Marian Hooper's trip to Washington to see the parades of war heroes may seem naive today, but in 1865 she was doing what she could to show her appreciation of the sacrifices of the soldiers. Henry Adams could not take part in these celebrations because he would remain a private secretary in England until 1868. But he would have been vulnerable to the idea of the hero, too, particularly because of his habit of mind of finding heroes for himself.

Like most of his contemporaries, he voted for Grant in the Presidential election of 1868.[9] He did so, he said, because the military hero represented the rule of law and order. That is, he voted for a man who had been able to fulfill a symbolic role during the war. Grant had made his reputation as a man of determination partly by contrast with the vacillating generals who led the North during much of the war. Henry Adams, like many others, thought that the determination he had shown in the war would give him sterling character in the Presidency. Adams had reason to value this quality, for determination was certainly one of the qualities that John Quincy Adams had possessed in abundance. Before the Civil War Grant's handling of the problems of civilian life had not been impressive; of course Adams and his countrymen should have looked closely at a man whose ability to manage his businesses was so obviously limited. But neither Adams nor the rest of the country was disposed to ask many questions; after all, the possession of a genuine hero contributed much to self-esteem.

Adams's emotions were vulnerable, but his intellect was not. He saw soon after the election of Grant that persons like Charles Francis Adams were not to receive office in the new government. By any standard of judgment the country owed much to him, for he had kept the English out of the war while Grant was finishing off the South. But the fact that the venal interests operating in Washington in 1868 felt no need to reward the former diplomat were clearly visible to Adams's journalistic eye, and he knew the influences operating on Grant. Hero swiftly turned into antihero.

Adams gives Grant an entire chapter in the *Education*. Grant's greatest sin for Adams was not his venality, which Adams suspected but never proved. But his stupidity he found intolerable. The only other man like him that he had met was Garibaldi, whom Adams gave credit for slightly more intelligence than Grant. Yet, he says, "in both, the intellect counted for nothing; only the energy counted. The type was pre-intellectual, archaic, and would have seemed so even to the cave-dwellers."[10] Grant's manner of expressing himself was distasteful to a person as sensitive to literary nuances as was Adams: "He resorted, like most men of the same intellectual calibre, to commonplaces when at a loss for expression: 'Let us have peace': or 'The best way to treat a bad law is to execute it.' "[11] And yet this man was immensely popular with most Americans. The country that sets up and keeps such a leader has to feel in itself some of his qualities, and Adams knew very well what his vote for Grant implied. A leader could ennoble or demean those who followed him, and Adams pessimistically reflected, "The progress of evolution from President Washington to President Grant, was alone evidence enough to upset Darwin."[12] The wound to Adams's idealism in the matter of President Grant must have been severe, for it was about this time that he wrote "The New York Gold Conspiracy." This article, he knew, would send him into the opposition, and would make impossible obtaining any favors from the administration. But he persisted, and retreated from Washington in the summer of 1871. While away in England he received the offer of an assistant professorship of history at Harvard. He at first declined, but when it was offered again he accepted and began a new career.

III   *Teacher*

Adams's chapter about his professorship at Harvard is entitled "Failure," and the tone of the chapter confirms his pessimism. "The seven years he passed in teaching seemed to him lost."[13] he says, and "of all his many educations, Adams thought that of the schoolteacher the thinnest."[14] Statements like these have produced many counterstatements from the academics who now guard the Adams reputation. They have proved what Adams doubtless knew, that by the standards of the academy Adams was quite successful. He was an early user of the seminar method which had been in vogue at the German universities, and he thereby had great influence on the teaching of history in American universities. Some of his students, such as Henry Cabot Lodge and Henry Osborne Taylor, had vast influence both on the political and the academic worlds. So of course his failure was not absolute.

But Adams had a strong sense of idealism about education, and he could not be satisfied by mediocrity. One of his most famous epigrams is: "A teacher affects eternity; he can never tell where his influence stops."[15] Granted that Adams's statement of the case is accurate, then the responsibilities of the teacher become infinite. Only action that meets the standards of the categorical imperative can suffice. With infinite responsibility, the teacher can hardly be expected to succeed absolutely. Torn between the demands of his idealization and the sober reality that every teacher must experience, Adams retreated. The knowledge that any statement about education must be somewhat ironical gave him protection.

In his special function as teacher of history, Adams says that the teacher "must either treat history as a catalogue, a record, a romance or an evolution."[16] Although he professes himself to have no theory of evolution in history to teach, he feels that the lack was itself a problem. He sees that the difficulty was greatest in medieval history, the field in which he taught for a time: "He knew better than though he were a professional historian that the man who should solve the riddle of the Middle Ages and bring them into the line of evolution from past to present, would be a greater man than Lamarck or Linnaeus."[17] But history seemed not to care. By comparison with the sciences, it was a hundred years behind. "Since Gibbon," he says, "the spectacle was almost a scandal."[18]

IV Success

The *Education* skips from the early years of teaching medieval history at Harvard to a period twenty years later, 1892. Many critics have puzzled over this omission of what would seem the most successful period of his life—the period of the biographies and the novels and the monumental history of the Jefferson and Madison administrations. Some have felt that his thesis of failure would be contradicted by an account of success enough for several lifetimes. Others have seen in it a suppression of the events leading up to and following the suicide of Marian Adams. But neither seems necessary, for the story that Adams is telling in the *Education* goes directly from the formulation of the problem in "Failure" to his attempts to solve the problem when he took it up again in the sixth decade of his life. However ironical he may have been about his search for form, this gap was not one of his problems.

In the introductory chapter in which Adams reviews his own condition and that of the country in 1892, he mentions the sculpture which he had commissioned St. Gaudens to execute for his plot in Rock Creek Cemetry in Washington.[19] The hooded figure would have been intelligible to any Asiatic, he averred, but it was nearly unintelligible to Americans. Adams sometimes amused himself by watching the puzzlement of those who came to look at the monument. His attitude of superiority makes him seem unpleasant to his readers, but as is so often the case with Adams an irony lurks nearby. For all his knowledge he is little better than his fellow Americans, most of whom have lost their sense of values. Adams is different from them only in that he is seeking education—seeking a set of symbols adequate to sustain faith, as Chartres had once sustained faith in the Middle Ages.

A glimmering came to him at the Chicago Exposition of 1893, where he went after being threatened for months by the financial panic of that year. Adams had been fascinated by money symbolism since his secretaryship in England during the Civil War. He could see that Americans cared little for money, despite their preoccupation with getting it.[20] The Chicago Exposition was something more than a gaudy display of wealth. It was the first time Americans had arranged a mechanical sequence which was capable of suggesting a direction of development.[21] It was "the first expression of American thought as a unity."[22] The symbolism of science so overwhelmed him that he took up the old post of meditating in Rome before the symbols which had enabled Gibbon to conceive of his great history: "One sat down to ponder on the steps beneath Richard Hunt's dome almost as deeply as on the steps of Ara Coeli, and much to the same purpose."[23] But the symbols he saw in Chicago were very different from those of Ara Coeli or Chartres. They were symbols of energy and force, and Adams felt that the country's commitment to capitalism in opting for gold in 1893 confirmed their importance for the country. Clearly, he is suggesting that minds which choose this kind of symbolism are more akin to the Roman, than the Christian aspect of Ara Coeli.

At the Paris Exposition of 1900, Adams found confirmation of the importance of the symbols he had noticed first at Chicago seven years earlier. In the dynamo he found a "symbol of infinity" which he felt "as a moral force, much as the early Christians felt the Cross." And in the end he began to pray to it.[24] Obviously, Adams is being ironical: he is expressing the fact that he understands the dynamo as a phenomenon and feels its importance at the same time. He is offering himself as a man of his time, who feels this symbol because it expresses ideas "that are in the air," as Whitehead put it. There is a reciprocal arrangement between himself and the symbol: he must choose it because it is one of the things his age puts before him, but he is free to feel it or not, as he has education to understand and sensitivity to feel.

He compares his situation with that of the followers of the Virgin. She too was a symbol: "She was goddess because of her force; she was the animated dynamo; she was reproduction—the greatest and most mysterious of all energies; all she needed was to be fecund."[25] Though brought up among the Puritans, Adams could understand that she had been one of the most efficacious forces for the stimulation of human energies that had ever existed. Adams by training had been deprived of her influence, just as his idol Gibbon had been. If Gibbon could find the symbols of Rome adequate to stimulate him to creating a unity as great as his history, perhaps the dynamo could be adequate for Adams.

In two chapters of the *Education*, "A Dynamic Theory of History" and "A Law of Acceleration," Adams brings together the material he thought would solve the problem of twentieth-century multiplicity. Adams evidently thought these chapters among the most important of his book, for he claimed that he had had like St. Augustine and Rousseau a didactic purpose, but that like them he had failed to find a satisfactory form for its expression.[26] If Samuels is right, however, in reading the book as a quest, these chapters form a triumphant conclusion. Adams had solved the problem of placing the Middle Ages into a system of history, and he is able to project an interpretation that will permit men to cope with the future. The small concluding chapter, "Nunc Age," is dénouement; even the *Libestod* does not conclude at its highest pitch of intensity. Of course, if one reads Adams's theory as his own confession of failure, then the quest is a failure and *Chartres* is simply a guidebook and the *Education* is merely autobiography. But only the careless could read them so.

The fundamental concept for Adams's theory of history is the supremacy of mind: again and again he insists on man's ability to conceptualize as the key to the solution of his problem.[27] The concept which he chooses to follow through history is that of force, which he places both in the external world and in man's own mind. Force is both physical and mental. Primitive man conceptualized the idea of unity from himself; he then projected it outward onto the part of the universe that was not himself. Man in his capacity as symbol-maker conceived the idea of the unity of the universe, and he called it God.

Unable to understand the concept of force, man symbolized it.[28] This ability led him to acquire to a very great degree the power to pursue force, an ability brought to high development in the ancient world. But then the Roman Empire broke down, for no apparent reason. Adams, again at Ara Coeli pondering, could offer only the thought that the Empire had developed too much energy too fast.[29] By this statement Adams would seem to be saying that Rome developed beyond the capacity of its symbols to concentrate and organize force. When the leading symbols of the age ceased to appeal to the minds of men, their energies could no longer be concentrated upon the problems of the age.

Rome was followed by another symbol which served for a very long time: the Christian cross.[30] Its power was as real to those who believed in it as energy is to the modern scientist. During the Middle Ages the mind that was energized by the cross expressed itself in many ways—cathedrals, sculpture, and poetry, among other things. The habit of mind of referring all things to the idea of religious unity was to persist long after the Middle Ages. The great scientists of the seventeenth century were all religious men who referred everything to the idea of unity. But with Lord Bacon, Adams thought, came a reversal of thought and force. The latter was allowed free development, a fact which accounts for the runaway development of force by the year 1900.

Adams, evidently frightened by the enormous increases in the use of energy in the nineteenth century and particularly by their extrapolation into the future, proposes that man must change: he must get back to thought's controlling force. He suggests a poetic solution: "The image needed here is that of a new centre, or preponderating mass, artificially introduced on earth in the midst of a system of attractive forces that previously made their own equilibrium, and constantly induced to accelerate its motion till it shall establish a new equilibrium."[31] He suggests the image of a comet,[32] which makes its way toward the sun, apparently destined for destruction, and then reverses itself to move with vertiginous speed upon the opposite course. Because men have already learned to operate with the law of contradiction, it should not be impossible for them to establish once more the ascendancy of mind. Adams, then, despite all that has been written about his pessimism, turns out to be an optimist. The energy crisis for his time was certainly what seemed an irreversible problem, but Adams knew it was not. He had seen the efficacy of the symbol at Chartres, and he knew that even the energies of the twentieth century could be brought under its control. But he did not propose what that symbol should be. It is just possible that his manikin could himself be the symbol needed; capacious enough of mind to understand the movement of history, yet driven by his weakness to a sense of his own humility, he might serve as a symbol of the kind of man needed for the age.

V *Evaluation*

The *Education* is Adams's best known as well as his greatest book. The relevance to modern life of so much of its material and its epigrammatic style have made it one of the most often quoted books in the language. One of its episodes has even been made into poetry: Robert Lowell's "Henry Adams 1850" is based on Adams's description of his play as a twelve-year-old boy.[33] Lowell's best contribution is his allowing the boy to characterize his own mind as "disquieting." The ability to see so deeply and to understand so quickly gave him the capacity to reveal the potential for good and for evil in those around him, but especially in himself. His ceaseless wandering to the far places of the earth, his endless study, his enormous correspondence are all attempts to understand himself. The *Education* shows his disquiet more clearly than any other of his books, and it is the most disquieting and therefore the richest of his writings.

Because the *Education* was published after Adams's death, he did not prepare it for the press. Had he done so, he would surely have omitted the subtitle, "An Autobiography," which was added to Adams's original wording. This original misreading must have led to many others, though it is easy enough to think of the book as autobiography. But Adams makes it clear that he is writing about a "manikin," a puppet of less than full human dimensions. And his handling of form, with the twenty-year hiatus in the middle and the inconclusive conclusion, tell the reader he is not reading conventional autobiography.

But as the story of a man's search for an adequate set of symbols, the book is great. Henry Adams is Everyman in the modern world, immersed in an ocean of symbols, desperately trying to determine which are relevant to his condition. Again and again the manikin tilts at his windmills and comes away bloody. His idealization of Grant, his hope of saving the world from the vantage point of a professor's or an editor's chair, his worship of the dynamo, all reveal expectations that show the manikin as hopelessly out of step with his time as was Don Quixote. Again and again the manikin is made ludicrous, but at the same time he reveals the flaws in society as well. Adams's ability to render the richness and complexity of this comedy that cuts both ways at once makes the *Education* one of the most interesting of twentieth-century American books.

CHAPTER 11

Theorist of History

B ROOKS ADAMS credits John Quincy Adams with being the
source of the interest in science which he and Henry shared.[1]
The *Education* tells of the glasses turned over caterpillars and of
experiments in the garden at Quincy. Both boys had heard of the
"Report on Weights and Measures" which their grandfather had
written while he was Secretar, of State, and they had heard of his
interest in the establishment of an observatory. These interests
caused Brooks and Henry Adams to call their grandfather's thought
"scientific," though the term did not fit very precisely. But the
grandfather's attitudes were important for education, and his grand-
sons' interest in science continued throughout their careers.

In the middle of the nineteenth century, when Henry Adams was
beginning his education, much of the new scientific thought had an
historical emphasis: Lyell's studies in geology stressed the great age
of the earth and Darwin's theories postulated the development over
a long period of time of the plants and animals of the earth. Adams
was exposed to this kind of thinking as an undergraduate at Harvard
when he attended Agassiz's lectures on paleontology.[2] There Adams
learned to stress the catastrophic in his interpretation of change, an
idea which Agassiz had developed in his observations concerning
the effect of glaciation. Even though Adams was soon to encounter
theories of uniformitarian development, he always retained some
disposition toward the catastrophic.

In England during the Civil War, he was drawn into contact with
many English intellectuals. Here, too, he found the relationship of
science and history close. In 1865 he encountered the ideas of Auguste Comte, in their popularization by John Stuart Mill.[3] Comte's
interpretation of the development of human institutions postulated
an early theological stage, shading over into a metaphysical period,

and ending in a positive or sceintific stage. Though Adams professed interest in Comte's theory, he did not use it slavishly in his own writing of history. But he retained his interest in it sufficiently to include it in some of his theorizing about historical process in his old age.

Adams's return to Comte suggests that he had retained some of the habits of mind of the mid-Victorian. Comte had relied more on analogy than on experimentation for his generalizations, and Adams did likewise. He searched through dozens of volumes of scientific works, not for what they had to say about a particular problem, but for their bearing on the question of history. As Joseph Mindel has suggested, Adams was interested in the metaphoric relationship of history to science, an interest which might have led him to discover some of the metaphoric assumptions of the scientists, had he known enough.[4] But his main interest was not in science, but history. His theoretical essays were all efforts to influence other practitioners of his craft, to shake them out of a complacency that, since Gibbon, was "practically a scandal."[5]

I *Movement in History*

The first of Adams's theoretical papers devoted to the philosophy of history was "The Tendency of History," which was read at the meeting of the American Historical Association in 1894.[6] Adams had been elected vice-president of the association in 1890. Despite his failure to attend meetings, he was reelected in 1892 and was named president in 1893. Because he was too shy to address a large public meeting, he prepared a paper instead. It was read for him as the presidential address of the Association.

The problem Adams raised for his fellow historians was that of the possibility of developing a science of history.[7] The expectations raised by the work of Buckle and Darwin, he said, had brought an immense amount of work which had created a mass of new insights. That this effort should not yet have raised history to the level of a science should not deter those who are still striving to find the generalization that will fix cause and effect in history. Adams confessed to apprehension at the discovery of such a principle, for he knew that it would necessarily be disruptive. Rousseau, Adam Smith, and Darwin had all created dissention. The discovery of a new principle in history might well set historians against powerful social organizations. If so, historians must not flinch from telling the truth.

Adams's second attempt to focus the attention of his brethren in history onto the problems brought on them by the advance of science came to naught. The American Historical Association declined to publish his "Rule of Phase Applied to History"; but the essay was included in the book *The Degradation of the Democratic Dogma,* which Brooks Adams published after Henry's death. Adams averred that "the future of Thought, and therefore of History, lies in the hands of the physicists, and . . . the future historian must seek his education in the world of mathematical physics."[8] Adams sought to apply from the Rule of Phase as formulated by Willard Gibbs a theory which would satisfy this need of the historian to go to the physicist as the leader in thought. Adams satisfied himself, though practically no one else, that he had done so. He worked out a series of phases in history, which he saw as beginning in fetish force, then moving into mechanical force, then electric force, and finally ethereal force. Noting the increasingly short duration of each phase, he derived mathematically the idea that the limits of thought would be reached in 1917, or at the very most, after generous allowances, 2025.

A great deal of critical ink has been spilled to prove Adams a scientific ignoramus who did not understand Gibbs at all. But Adams's inclination toward comedy would make it seem as if he were laying a trap for the slow-witted historian. He knew very well the limitations of the scientific method for history, but he also knew that lesser minds in the humanities were all too ready to cash in on the prestige of the sciences. Their stretching history on the Procrustean bed of physics was exactly like his mathematical interpretation of the movement of thought. If, like a Swift, he could get the historians to see the errors of their ways, he would have won something for the writing of history as a record of human activity.

II   A Letter to American Teachers of History

In February 1910 Adams sent printed copies of *A Letter to American Teachers of History* to a number of historians, requesting in a prefatory letter that they examine the argument and respond if they chose. Few responded, and the document has never attracted much favorable notice. One who did answer was Frederick Jackson Turner, one of the strongest advocates of the use of scientific techniques in the writing of history.[9] Yet he sneered at Adams's *Letter.* Today his sneer seems defensive; Turner must have known what a frail reed the "frontier thesis" was, even when it seemed to provide a "scientific" explanation for the development of America. He could never risk Adams's frank and bold use of analogy, which could make a parody of all "scientific" thinking in history.

Adams gives over the first part of his essay to explaining the problem brought about by the second law of thermodynamics, which states that entropy in the universe tends to a maximum.[10] Obviously, this problem is not merely one on which analogies between science and history can be built: it is itself a statement about history. The problems of the extreme wastefulness of the sun and of its ultimate extinction operate with such slowness as to be of no practical concern to men presently on earth, as Adams readily admits. Yet for historians who had not long before been advocating a doctrine of unlimited progress, this idea provides a severe check. On one level entropy might work the historian mischief by replacing his positive goals with absolute extinction. And Adams carries this idea a step further by suggesting that social energy might also tend to a maximum of entropy.

Although it would seem that society believed as strongly as ever in its old doctrine of progress, Adams notes a number of statistics that point to the opposite.[11] He cites the number of suicides, the increase of alcoholism, the increase of disease as signs of loss of vitality in the body politic. And a number of the currently fashionable philosophies all tend toward pessimism. Yet, Adams points out that a historian offering a set of lectures as pessimistic as the scientists postulate would be dismissed from the university. Historians have always taught according to the doctrine of progress, even when progress was not apparent. Man cannot take lightly the denial of this doctrine by the scientist:

Somewhere he will have to make a stand, but he has been already so much weakened by the surrender of his defences that he knows no longer where a stand can be made. As a form of Vital Energy he is convicted of being a Vertebrate, a Mammal, a Monodelphe, a Primate, and must eternally, by his body, be subject to the second law of thermodynamics. Escape there is impossible. Science has shut and barred every known exit. Man can detect no outlet except through the loophole called Mind, and even to avail himself of this, he must follow Lapparent's advice,—become a disembodied spirit and seek a confederate among such physicists or physiologists as are willing to admit that man, as an animal, has no importance; that his evolution or degradation as an organism is immaterial; that his physical force or condition has nothing to do with the subject; that the old ascetics were correct in surpressing the body; and that his consciousness is sufficient proof of his right to regard Reason as the highest potential of Vital Energy.[12]

In philosophy, Adams points out, this idea goes back to Aristotle, but for his immediate purpose he prefers to call attention to Schopenhauer's identification of the energy of nature with will.

He then examines a great many scientific interpretations of the place of will and thought in the modern consciousness, and concludes, "If this is the best that physiology and metaphysics can do to help the historian of man, the outlook is far from cheerful."[13] Their attempt to link thought with the mechanical processes of the universe and therefore with the possibility of degradation is repugnant to the historian. For him, "the function of man is the the production of Thought."[14] If the production of man is mere instinct instead of thought, then the historian has nothing of importance to do. Adams asserts categorically: "The University, as distinct from the technological school, had no proper function other than to teach that the flower of vital energy is Thought, and that not Instinct but Intellect is the highest power of a supernatural Will;—an intimate, independent, self-producing, self-sustaining, incorruptible solvent of all earlier or lower energies, and incapable of degradation or dissolution."[15]

The final section of Adams's treatise is presented as a series of arguments, on the one hand for the degradationists or the scientists, and on the other for the evolutionists or the historians. Adams allows the degradationist to indict man for his wastefulness of coal, oil, gas, peat, wood, and oxygen. Man's pleasure seem often quite unintelligent: drinking alcohol, burning fireworks, or firing cannon.[16] The evolutionist cannot deny these charges, but he replies that the generation of thought in the process of man's life on the planet gives man a far more valuable resource than the commodities he has dissipated. When the evolutionist concedes that thought, too, may be subject to the dissipation of its energies, he hopes to get the concession that vital energy can maintain its tension by contracting its volume like the sun. But the scientist feels that the failure of the evolutionist to make mind a separate entity vitiates his argument. For him the highest intensities in the scale came at the beginning, when the atom and the molecule were produced. To him reason seems much less intense, and even reason has declined in energy since its highest achievement in the Gothic cathedrals. Adams feels that no reconciliation of the positions is possible, but he adds: "The contradiction between science and instinct is so radical that, though science should prove twenty times over, by every method of demonstration known to it, that man is a thermodynamic mechanism, instinct would reject the proof, and whenever it should be convinced, it would have to die."[17] Adams believes that compromise of principle is impossible, and that the next step in the controversy is direct conflict. Each may try to assert his freedom to choose, regardless of the underlying logic. The professor of history can show how man has learned to control by his reason all the forces which have come into his purview since 1830.[18] Yet Adams feels that the physicists will answer that the theory of tropism requires the admission that physical energies tend to absorb psychical energies. But the historians and sociologists cannot admit that gains in power are made at the expense of human vitality. Again, both sides are far from effecting a meeting of minds.

Adams turns to a weakness in the scientists' arguments: their inability to answer the question of origin.[19] By shrouding the beginnings, they obscure the entire picture of development. Kelvin gave himself at the beginning all the power he needed, so that his system could furnish its own momentum for degradation. And the idea of unity itself gives the degradationist an unfair advantage. Adams concedes the convenience of the idea of unity, but he points out that simplicity is not necessarily truth. Yet, because man has an intuitive desire for unity, the scheme of the degradationists appeals to his imagination, and the scheme which shows everything tending to entropy is easily acceptable because it can be so neatly formulated.

The historian, expressing the desires of the popular mind, might fix on the idea that society is tending toward equilibrium.[20] But the scientists show that equilibrium is death. The historian cannot choose to leave his human material at the level of the ants and bees; instead, he must, if he is going to carry his audience with him, adopt the view of society's rising to a level of high potential energy. But this view does not satisfy the classical university teacher of history, because he wants to exercise his customary intuitions of free will and art.

The professor of history in this situation is very nearly in the

position of being an anachronism. Some of the scientists see the
possibility of the development of science only as long as there is no
history. He is in an especially bad state, Adams says, in that "the law
of entropy imposes a servitude on all energies, including the mental. The degree of freedom steadily and rapidly diminishes. Without
rest, the physicists gently push history down the decline, as yet
scarcely conscious, which they are certain to plot out by abscissae
and ordinates as soon as they can fix and agree upon a sufficient
number of normal variables, not with conscious intention but by
unconscious extension."[21] The scientists mock present-day society
by citing statistics that point to degradation. The historian, trying to
get some amelioration of this tendency to help him in his function of
teaching the young, can get from the scientist only the concession
that degradation may sometimes convey the impression of progress.
But behind this impression of order really lies the absence of power
to do work, that is, death. The scientist makes pessimism the logical
foundation upon which optimism can rest. Adams says, "History is
the victim of both."[22]

He goes on to condemn some of the more recent views of history:

In short, the social Organism, in the recent views of history, is the cause,
creator, and end of the Man, who exists only as a passing representative of
it, without rights or functions except what it imposes. As an Organism,
society has always been peculiarly subject to degradation of Energy, and
alike the historians and the physicists invariably stretch Kelvin's law over all
organized matter whatever. Instead of being a mere convenience in treatment, the law is very rapidly becoming a dogma of absolute Truth. As long
as the theory of Degradation,—as of Evolution,—was only one of the con-
venient tools of science, the sociologist had no just cause for complaint.
Every science,—and mathematics first of all, uses what tools it likes.[23]

Adams sees that some mode must be developed to enable professors
in all disciplines to teach about the working of physico-chemical and
mechanical energies. But he feels that scientists who deal with humanity

will find great difficulty in agreeing on any formula which does not require
from physics the abandonment, in part, of the second law of thermodynamics. The mere formal exception of Reason from the express operation of the law, as a matter of teaching in the workshop, is not enough.
Either the law must be abandoned in respect to Vital Energy altogether, or

Vital Energy must abandon Reason altogether as one of its forms, and return to the old dilemma of Descartes.[24]

Adams then concludes that each university may first have to work out its problem for itself, and this step would make a good beginning. But for a complete solution of the problem, he feels the difficulty may require the aid of another Newton.

III *Evaluation*

Adams's theoretical essays about the tendency of history have all too often been taken as the dabblings of an old man who pretended to more knowledge of science than he possessed. His detractors have had no difficulty proving his ignorance of many of the niceties of the scientific materials he used. But they have overstressed these details and have often failed to heed the purpose and tone of his essays. All too often Adams has been interpreted as the advocate of the writing of scientific history complete with a suitable philosophy of determinism. True, Adams wanted to raise the prestige of history to the level of a science, but he knew that if it could eventually be so classified, it would not be mathematical or deterministic in the way of the sciences. In none of his essays does he offer a program for the writing of history; rather, he takes the role of the seeker who attempts to focus the attention of younger scholars on questions that need solution.

In the final quarter of the twentieth century, Adams has once again come into popular notice, this time for his ideas about entropy. Writers like William Pynchon usually interpret Adams as a pessimist, as indeed the idea of entropy would seem to require. Adams was indeed unhappy with the implications of entropy for the human race, but he was not one to concede defeat easily. When he said that another Newton may be necessary to save the world, he was not being despairingly ironical. A Newton would represent an extreme concentration of the power of thought, and Adams had all along sought to place the energy of thought in the same scale as physical energy. But so far the world has not been able to see the problem in this way, and it remembers Adams, not for his solution, but for his presentation of the problem of entropy.

CHAPTER 12

The Life of George Cabot Lodge

A DAMS wrote his last book as a memorial to his young friend the
poet George Cabot Lodge, the son of Massachusetts senator
Henry Cabot Lodge.[1] Adams had known the elder Lodge as a student at Harvard and as his assistant on the *North American Review*,
and he had traveled to Europe with the Lodge family in 1895, when
he began the study that would lead to *Mont-Saint-Michel and
Chartres.* "Bay" Lodge, as the son was called, traveled with his
family on this trip, and the relationship between him and Adams
soon ripened into that of disciple and master. Although their personal contact was interrupted by the peregrinations and responsibilities of both, their friendship continued until Lodge's death in
1909 at the age of thirty-six. When the Lodge family decided upon
the publication of Bay's poetry and plays as a memorial, Adams was
selected to write a biography as a companion volume. This was a
difficult assignment, for Adams knew that Lodge's poetry did not
measure up to the highest standard.

He adopted a characteristic Adams stance as his most important
device for solving his problem: he took an Olympian tone which
precluded any descent into sentimentality and which allowed him to
comment only as much as he desired.[2] In a manner somewhat like
that of the *Education*, he interprets young Lodge as a person formed
by and yet reacting against the New England environment. Adams
dwells upon the responsibilities of being a Cabot, a Davis, a Mills,
and a Lodge all at once, and explains his friend's escape into poetry
as an effort to find himself. Lodge wrote in some of his earliest
poetry about the energies of nature; in "The Wave," Adams says,
"he did not invent images for amusement, but described himself in
describing the energy."[3] This attitude, Adams feels, could not be
understood in Boston, which had always had the practical problem
of making its way against a hostile nature. Adams's explanation
128

suffices for Lodge's failure to appeal to the workmen or businessmen of Boston, but it does not explain the problem of Lodge's personifications, which now seem weakly Byronic:

> And the wave called to its brothers,
> "This is the crest of life!"[4]

Probably Adams did not see how Lodge's mind was not nearly as strong as his own; Lodge could only take the stamp of his education—unlike Adams, who always imprinted himself on his materials.

Education at Harvard College followed the conventional New England plan, where young Lodge conscientiously tried to follow the discipline prescribed for him. He read enormously, and the desire to read led to the desire to write. By some contrariety of his nature, Adams thinks, Lodge began with the Petrarchan sonnet: he "had plunged headlong into the higher problems of literary art, before he was fairly acquainted with the commoner standards."[5] Adams implies, though he does not say so precisely, that this beginning with the difficult and Lodge's constantly eschewing the English model for the foreign may have been at the root of his difficulty. For when at the end of his Harvard education he went to Paris, he found himself in great difficulty, despite his consuming ambition. Lodge was able to persist and to gain something, but Adams's comment about the quality of his French education seems anything but approving: "Thousands of young people, of both sexes, pass through the same experience in their efforts to obtain education, in Paris or elsewhere, and are surprised to find at the end, that their education consists chiefly in whatever many-colored impressions they have accidentally or unconsciously absorbed."[6] Neither does Adams approve of Lodge's spending the winter of 1896–97 in Berlin, which, his own memories taught him, was "a grave strain on the least pessimistic temper."[7] Lodge made little of his experience, for he had gone to read Schopenhauer, who, Adams observes, "can be studied anywhere."[8] Lodge did a great deal of solitary hard labor in his years abroad. Yet even this loneliness may have been a disadvantage, for it caused him to publish, before he was sure of himself, his first volume of poems, *The Song of the Wave*. Adams quite correctly dismisses most of the poems in the volume, commenting, "Such work marks the steps of study and attainment rather than attainment itself."[9]

After a short tour of duty with the navy during the Spanish-American War, marriage, and another European tour, Lodge settled down to the literary work which filled the latter part of his life. In this period he concentrated on the drama, in which he took his ideas from Schopenhauer. Adams explains that his central motif was "the idea of Will, making the universe, but existing only as subject. The Will is God; it is nature; it is all that is; but it is knowable only as ourself. Thus the sole tragic action of humanity is the Ego,—the Me,—always maddened by the necessity of self-sacrifice, the superhuman effort of lifting himself and the universe by sacrifice."[10] Lodge's choice of matter, Adams feels, had "the supreme merit of being the most universal tragic motive on the whole possible range of thought."[11] Yet Lodge's treatment, Adams thinks, suffered from the fault of exuberance. And this quality caused him to exceed the bounds of *mesure*. This is Adams's most telling criticism of Lodge's work, and it applies not only to his dramas but to his poems as well. He is a poet and dramatist of the exclamation point. That he could have used this crutch for so long suggests an incredible lack of maturity. He illustrates all too clearly Emerson's warning against overdependence on vicarious experience. The years at Harvard, in Paris, in Berlin, and on the beaches at Nahant and Tuckanuck had produced ample store of intellectual fare, but, it would seem, all too little feeling.

In the drama *Cain*, Lodge shows how man is under the necessity of asserting his freedom of will or of submitting to destiny. To develop his idea, Lodge uses only four characters: Cain, Abel, Adam, and Eve. He makes Adam a weakling; he leaves Abel undeveloped; he works Cain up to a pitch of insanity. But Eve is his truly sympathetic character, and she ends by assuming the burden of Cain. Adams suggests that Eve's force is such that perhaps the drama ought to be named for her. Yet whatever its faults, he believes that in all of American literature there is not "another dramatic effort as vigorous and sustained as that of *Cain*."[12]

Although Lodge seemed so strong in youth, he became aware some time after his marriage of the precariousness of his health. This knowledge gave him a new theme—that of doubt—but he had no time to develop its potential.[13] Instead, he concentrated his energies on the drama *Herakles*, a work which nearly equaled in bulk all of his other writings combined. This play reinterprets the Greek story as related by the historian Diodorus; its theme—the sacrifice of a god for a world of which he himself is a part—had preoccupied the mind of Lodge throughout his writing career.

Lodge's play makes Herakles a rather self-righteous, messianic figure who eventually kills his children. Adams describes his actions as "insanity," but admits that on the handling of this scene the standing of the dramatist must depend.[14] Adams finally admits that Lodge failed to make Herakles' motives convincing, though he declares that his own doubts about the dramatist's ability to handle this scene led to self-doubt in the critic. For Adams the killing of the children is the climax of Lodge's drama. Unfortunately for this interpretation, the dramatist did not proceed with his dénouement. Instead, he undertook to resolve the philosophical problem brought about by the freeing of Prometheus. Lodge interpreted the problem as a part of the general question of man's freedom, which he resolved by postulating that freedom is a good in itself.[15] However congenial this idea may be to Adams, he is unable to reconcile it with the other strand in the drama and he finally declares himself unsatisfied.

I *Evaluation*

Adams's *Lodge* has been called a cold book,[16] but this surely is not the case; rather it is a judicious book, remarkable for its ability to suggest the distant, rarefied affection of an old intellectual for a much younger person. Adams used Lodge's own letters to build up a convincing picture of an exuberant, rather overprotected young man, pathetically cut off in youth despite all that wealth, position, and training could do for him. Against this emotional side of the book Adams set the intellectual, where he took the part of the critic who looked carefully and sympathetically at the writings themselves. He showed appreciation as far as was possible, but he did not withhold reservations when they seemed necessary. The pity of Adams's book is that its subject was so slight and that Adams was more than seventy when he first became a literary critic. If he had found a writer strong enough to hold his interest, he might have extended his fame to still another field.

CHAPTER 13

The Impact of Henry Adams

THE famous epigram, "A teacher affects eternity; he can never tell where his influence stops," could well be used to describe the influence of its author. Certainly it is impossible at this point to see an end to Adams's influence. Because of the current energy crisis, parts of the *Education* have become once again almost as timely as the newspaper. His ideas about entropy have become part of the material which Thomas Pynchon has used for his fiction. And the current interest in the application of the idea of entropy to other fields such as economics has given Adams a reputation as a thinker by no means confined to history or literature.

Adams's individual works have a solidity and vitality that enable them to endure. His *Life of Albert Gallatin*, published almost a hundred years ago, still receives respectful comments from scholars in the field. *John Randolph* is still lively enough to attract a wide reading audience. His *History of the United States during the Administrations of Jefferson and Madison* is ranked by Yvor Winters with Gibbon's *Decline and Fall of the Roman Empire*. If professional historians sometimes undervalue the literary qualities of Adams's *History*, they nonetheless give him credit for solid research and judicious presentation. *Mont-Saint-Michel and Chartres* and *The Education of Henry Adams* still command wide attention for their originality of form and for their striking content. Any one of these books would be sufficient to insure Adams a reputation; together they confirm him as the most important American historian of the nineteenth and twentieth centuries.

Because Adams so often compared himself with his famous ancestors, it is impossible not to think of his contribution as measured against theirs. Can the accomplishment of a mere scholar compare with John Adams's part in drawing up the Constitution, or John Quincy Adams's participation in the drawing up the Treaty of

Ghent, or of Charles Francis Adams's minimizing the British assistance to the Confederacy in the Civil War? If one were foolish enough to attempt to choose among them, he would have to decide all over again the problem of the man of action and the man of thought. Each of the men of action had his influence on the course of the nation and has his reputation as a continuing influence. But the hundreds of thousands who have read the books of Henry Adams have given him an influence which now seems likely to be unending.

Notes and References

Chapter One

1. *The Education of Henry Adams* (Boston and New York, 1918), p. 3.
2. James Truslow Adams, *The Adams Family* (Boston, 1931), pp. 4–7.
3. Ibid., pp. 26–115 *passim*.
4. Ibid., pp. 119–228 *passim*.
5. Ibid., pp. 231–302 *passim*.
6. Ibid., pp. 7–8.
7. *Education*, p. 16.
8. Ibid., pp. 12–14.
9. Ibid., pp. 54–69.
10. Ibid., p. 55.
11. Ernest Samuels, *The Young Henry Adams* (Cambridge, Massachusetts, 1948), pp. 16–32.
12. Ibid., pp. 12–16.
13. Ibid., pp. 51–52.
14. Ibid., pp. 53–54.
15. Ibid., pp. 55–56.
16. Ibid., pp. 61–63.
17. *Education*, pp. 91–92.
18. Samuels, *The Young Henry Adams*, pp. 81–82.
19. "The Great Secession Winter of 1860–61," *Proceedings of the Massachusetts Historical Society* 43 (1910), 656.
20. Ibid., 660–87.
21. Ibid., 665.
22. Ibid., 666.
23. Ibid., 686.

Chapter Two

1. Samuels, *The Young Henry Adams*, pp. 93–96.
2. Ibid., p. 97.
3. Ibid., pp. 115–19.
4. Ibid., pp. 122–25.
5. *Education*, p. 214.
6. Ibid., p. 142.
7. Samuels, *The Young Henry Adams*, p. 129.
8. The review appeared in the *North American Review* 107 (1868), 465–501.
9. *Education*, p. 230.

10. Ibid., p. 225.

11. John Stuart Mill, *Auguste Comte and Positivism* (Ann Arbor, 1961), pp. 10–15.

12. Samuels, *The Young Henry Adams*, p. 34.

13. Ibid., p. 135.

14. Ibid., pp. 134–35.

15. *Henry Adams and His Friends*, ed. Harold Dean Cater (Boston, 1947), pp. 8–10.

16. Ibid., pp. 14–15.

17. Charles F. Adams, Jr., and Henry Adams, "Captain John Smith," *Chapters of Erie, and Other Essays* (Boston, 1871), p. 192.

18. Grace Steele Woodward, *Pocahontas* (Norman, Oklahoma, 1969), p. 71n.

19. "Captain John Smith," pp. 198–222.

20. Samuels, *The Young Henry Adams*, pp. 168–78.

21. *Letters of Henry Adams* (1858–1891), ed. Worthington Chauncey Ford (Boston, 1930), p. 156.

22. *Education*, p. 271.

23. Samuels, *The Young Henry Adams*, pp. 195–96.

24. "The New York Gold Conspiracy," *Chapters of Erie, and Other Essays*, p. 100.

25. Ibid., p. 101.

26. Ibid., pp. 101–102.

27. Ibid., pp. 103–104.

28. Ibid., p. 104.

29. Ibid., p. 105.

30. Ibid., p. 107.

31. Ibid., p.111.

32. Ibid., p. 113.

33. Ibid., p. 115.

34. Ibid., pp. 117–27.

35. *Education*, p. 266.

36. Samuels, *The Young Henry Adams*, pp. 203–205.

37. *Education*, pp. 299–307.

38. Samuels, *The Young Henry Adams*, pp. 245–47.

39. "The Anglo-Saxon Courts of Law," *Essays in Anglo-Saxon Law* (Boston, 1876), pp. 1–2.

40. Ibid., p. 12.

41. Ibid., pp. 13–22.

42. Ibid., pp. 52–54.

43. Samuels, *The Young Henry Adams*, pp. 286–89.

44. Ibid., pp. 293–98.

45. *Education*, p. 225.

46. Sir Isaiah Berlin, *Four Essays on Liberty* (New York, 1969), p. 109.

Chapter Three

1. Ernest Samuels, *Henry Adams: The Middle Years* (Cambridge, Massachusetts, 1958), pp. 43–44.
2. *Letters* (1858–1891), p. 303.
3. See, for example, Raymond Walters, Jr., *Albert Gallatin* (New York, 1957), p. vii.
4. *The Life of Albert Gallatin* (Philadelphia, 1879), pp. 14–25.
5. Ibid., pp. 1–10.
6. Ibid., p. 25.
7. Ibid., p. 67.
8. Walters, *Albert Gallatin*, p. 27.
9. *The Life of Albert Gallatin*, p. 154.
10. Ibid., p. 171.
11. Ibid.
12. Ibid., p. 267.
13. Ibid., pp. 267–70.
14. Ibid., pp. 291–97.
15. Ibid., pp. 317–23.
16. Ibid., pp. 366–86.
17. Ibid., p. 368.
18. Ibid., pp. 385–98.
19. Ibid., p. 399.
20. Ibid., pp. 432–34.
21. Ibid., pp. 478–80.
22. Ibid., pp. 522–47.
23. Ibid., pp. 561–79.
24. Ibid., pp. 612–27.
25. Ibid., p. 638.
26. Ibid., p. 644.
27. Ibid., pp. 671–75.
28. *Letters* (1858–1891), p. 314.

Chapter Four

1. *Education*, p. 7.
2. Ibid., pp. 44–45.
3. Ibid., p. 57.
4. Samuels, *Henry Adams: The Middle Years*, p. 184.
5. *John Randolph* (Boston and New York, 1882), p. 6.
6. Ibid., p. 7.
7. Ibid., p. 10.
8. Ibid.
9. Ibid., p. 13.
10. Ibid., p. 14.

11. Ibid., pp. 18–20.
12. Ibid., p. 33.
13. Ibid., p. 32.
14. Ibid., p. 39.
15. Ibid., pp. 56–89.
16. Ibid., p. 90.
17. Ibid., pp. 67–73.
18. Ibid., pp. 95–99.
19. Ibid., pp. 130–51.
20. William C. Bruce, *John Randolph of Roanoke* (New York, 1922), I, 215.
21. *John Randolph*, p. 142.
22. Ibid., p. 172.
23. Ibid., p. 188.
24. Ibid., p. 202.
25. Ibid., p. 209.
26. Ibid., p. 210.
27. Ibid., p. 231.
28. Ibid., p. 234.
29. Ibid., p. 253.
30. Ibid., p. 259.
31. Ibid., p. 264.
32. Ibid., p. 286.
33. Ibid., p. 294.
34. Edward H. Carr, *What is History?* (New York, 1965), p. 26.
35. Russell Kirk, *John Randolph of Roanoke* (Chicago , 1964), p. 61.

Chapter Five

1. Samuels, *Henry Adams: The Middle Years*, p. 69.
2. John D. Hicks, *The American Nation* (Boston, 1941), pp. 53–55.
3. *Democracy* (New York, 1880), p. 136.
4. Ibid., p. 140.
5. Ibid., p. 141.
6. Ibid., pp. 160–61.
7. Ibid., pp. 182–83.
8. Ibid., p. 190.
9. Ibid., p. 213.
10. Ibid., pp. 325–39.
11. Ibid., pp. 42–43.
12. Ibid., p. 76.
13. Ibid., p. 77.
14. Ibid.
15. Ibid.
16. Ibid., p. 78.

17. Ibid.
18. Ibid., pp. 1–11.
19. Ibid., p. 10.
20. Ibid., p. 20.
21. Ibid., p. 26.
22. Ibid., pp. 36–37.
23. Ibid., p. 141.
24. Ibid., p. 144.
25. Ibid., p. 174.
26. Ibid., p. 374.

Chapter Six

1. *Esther* (New York, 1884), pp. 1–2.
2. Ibid., pp. 6–7.
3. Ibid., p. 7.
4. Ibid., p. 17.
5. Ibid., p. 20.
6. Ibid., p. 54.
7. Ibid., pp. 91–92.
8. Ibid., p. 21.
9. Ibid., p. 26.
10. Ibid., pp. 27–28.
11. Ibid., pp. 71–100.
12. Ibid., pp. 172–204.
13. Ibid., p. 211.
14. Ibid., pp. 241–302.
15. R. P. Blackmur, "Three Emphases on Henry Adams," *The Expense of Greatness* (Gloucester, Massachusetts, 1958), p. 263.

Chapter Seven

1. Samuels, *Henry Adams: The Middle Years*, pp. 111–42.
2. Ibid., pp. 259–89.
3. Ibid., pp. 290–348.
4. *History of the United States During the Administrations of Thomas Jefferson and James Madison* (New York, 1889–91), I, 40. This is the complete Scribner edition, which Adams published as a revision of his earlier, privately printed histories of the Jefferson and Madison administrations. This edition is much more conveniently available than the earlier publications.
5. Ibid., I, 86.
6. Ibid., I, 200.
7. Ibid., I, 202.
8. Ibid., I, 277.
9. Ibid.

10. Ibid., I, 277–78.
11. Ibid., I, 334.
12. Ibid., I, 378–98.
13. Ibid., II, 4–5.
14. Ibid., II, 39.
15. Ibid., II, 65.
16. Ibid., II, 91–92.
17. Ibid., II, 118.
18. Ibid., II, 125.
19. Berlin, *Four Essays on Liberty*, pp. 114–17.
20. *History*, III, 389–91.
21. Ibid., III, 392–440.
22. Ibid., IV, 1–26.
23. Ibid., IV, 103.
24. Ibid., IV, 138.
25. Ibid., IV, 139.
26. Ibid.
27. Ibid., IV, 271.
28. Ibid., IV, 277.
29. Ibid., IV, 454–55.
30. Ibid., V, 168.
31. Ibid., V, 169–75.
32. Ibid., V, 183.
33. Ibid., V, 182.
34. Ibid., V, 211–12.
35. Ibid., VI, 113.
36. Ibid., VI, 133–53.
37. Ibid., VI, 288.
38. Ibid., VI, 300.
39. Ibid., VI, 335.
40. Ibid., VI, 372.
41. Ibid., VI, 374–76.
42. Ibid., VII, 80.
43. Ibid., VII, 98.
44. Ibid., VII, 154–55.
45. Ibid., VII, 171.
46. Ibid., VII, 200.
47. Ibid., VII, 262.
48. Ibid., VII, 297.
49. Ibid., VII, 307.
50. Ibid., VII, 333.
51. Ibid., VIII, 45.
52. Ibid., VIII, 121.
53. Ibid., VIII, 123.

54. Ibid., VIII, 131.
55. Ibid., VIII, 153.
56. Ibid., IX, 154–218.
57. Ibid., IX, 219–42.
58. Samuels, *The Middle Years*, pp. 410–12.
59. Bradford Perkins, *Prologue to War: England and the United States, 1805–1812* (Berkeley and Los Angeles, 1961), p. 539.
60. John K. Mahon, *The War of 1812* (Gainesville, Florida, 1972), p. vii.
61. Yvor Winters, "Henry Adams, or the Creation of Confusion," *The Anatomy of Nonsense* (Norfolk, Connecticut, 1943), p. 85.
62. Berlin, *Four Essays on Liberty*, pp. 107–108.

Chapter Eight

1. *Letters (1858–1891)*, pp. 475–76.
2. Ibid., p. 488.
3. Ibid., pp. 487–88.
4. Ernest Samuels, *Henry Adams: The Major Phase* (Cambridge, Massachusetts, 1964), p. 100.
5. R. G. Collingwood, *The Idea of History* (New York, 1956), p. 9.
6. *Memoirs of Arii Taimai E.* (Paris, 1901), p. 136.
7. Ibid., p. 55.
8. Ibid., p. 56.
9. Ibid., p. 47.
10. Ibid., p. 136.
11. Ibid., pp. 62–97.
12. Ibid., p. 99.
13. Ibid., p. 101.
14. Ibid., pp. 101–106.
15. Ibid., p. 133.
16. Ibid., p. 142.
17. Ibid., p. 143.
18. Ibid.
19. Ibid., pp. 178–96.
20. Douglas L. Oliver, *Ancient Tahitian Society* (Honolulu, 1974), *passim*.

Chapter Nine

1. *Letters of Henry Adams (1892–1918)*, ed. Worthington Chauncey Ford (Boston, 1938), p. 78.
2. Harold Dean Cater, ed., *Henry Adams and His Friends*, p. xxiv.
3. *Letters (1858–1891)*, p. 434.
4. *Letters (1892–1918)*, pp. 332–33.
5. Ibid., p. 468.
6. Samuels, *Henry Adams: The Major Phase*, p. 214.

7. *Mont-Saint-Michel and Chartres* (Boston, 1913), p. 106.
8. Ibid., p. 1.
9. Ibid., pp. 6–7.
10. Ibid., pp. 10–11.
11. Ibid., p. 11.
12. Ibid., pp. 55–59.
13. Ibid., pp. 64–67.
14. Ibid., p. 68.
15. Ibid., p. 79.
16. Ibid., p. 99.
17. Ibid., p. 100.
18. Ibid., p. 128.
19. Ibid.
20. Ibid., p. 132.
21. Ibid., p. 134.
22. Ibid., p. 136.
23. Ibid., p. 176.
24. Bengt Danielsson, *Gaugin in the South Seas* (Garden City, New York, 1966), p. 97.
25. Ibid., pp. 62–63.
26. *Mont-Saint-Michel and Chartres*, p. 199.
27. Ibid., p. 210.
28. Ibid., p. 218.
29. Joseph Conrad, *Victory* (New York, 1921), p. 91.
30. *Mont-Saint-Michel and Chartres*, p. 226.
31. Ibid., p. 246.
32. Ibid.
33. Ibid., p. 241.
34. Ibid., pp. 292–303.
35. Ibid., p. 302.
36. Ibid., p. 304.
37. Ibid., p. 305.
38. Ibid., p. 315.
39. Ibid., p. 348.
40. Ibid., p. 376.
41. Ibid., p. 378.
42. Ibid., pp. 380–83.
43. Winters, *The Anatomy of Nonsense*, pp. 58–59.
44. Ibid., p. 64.

Chapter Ten

1. Samuels, *Henry Adams: The Major Phase*, p. 353.
2. *Education*, p. 8.
3. Ibid., pp. 12–13.

4. Ibid., pp. 47–48.
5. Samuels, *The Young Henry Adams*, pp. 8–52.
6. *Education*, p. 69.
7. Ibid., p. 149.
8. *Letters of Mrs. Henry Adams, 1865–1883*, ed. Ward Thoron (Boston, 1936), pp. 3–10.
9. *Education*, pp. 260–61.
10. Ibid., p. 265.
11. Ibid.
12. Ibid., p. 266.
13. Ibid., p. 304.
14. Ibid., p. 307.
15. Ibid., p. 300.
16. Ibid.
17. Ibid., p. 301.
18. Ibid.
19. Ibid., pp. 328–29.
20. Ibid., p. 328.
21. Ibid., p. 342.
22. Ibid., p. 343.
23. Ibid., p. 340.
24. Ibid., p. 380.
25. Ibid., p. 384.
26. *Letters (1892–1918)*, p. 490.
27. *Education*, p. 475.
28. Ibid., p. 476.
29. Ibid., p. 477.
30. Ibid., pp. 478–79.
31. Ibid., p. 489.
32. Ibid.
33. Robert Lowell, *History* (New York, 1973), p. 87.

Chapter Eleven

1. Brooks Adams, "The Heritage of Henry Adams," *The Degradation of the Democratic Dogma* (New York, 1919), pp. 1–122 *passim*.
2. *Education*, p. 60.
3. Ibid., p. 225.
4. Joseph Mindel, "The Uses of Metaphor: Henry Adams and the Symbols of Science," *Journal of the History of Ideas* 26 (1965), 101–102.
5. *Education*, p. 301.
6. Samuels, *Henry Adams: The Major Phase*, pp. 144–46.
7. *The Degradation of the Democratic Dogma*, pp. 126–27.
8. Ibid., p. 283.
9. Samuels, *Henry Adams: The Major Phase*, pp. 491–92.

10. *The Degradation of the Democratic Dogma*, pp. 140–50.
11. Ibid., pp. 186–90.
12. Ibid., pp. 191–92.
13. Ibid., p. 205.
14. Ibid.
15. Ibid., p. 206.
16. Ibid., p. 217.
17. Ibid., pp. 230–31.
18. Ibid., pp. 232–35.
19. Ibid., pp. 238–47.
20. Ibid., pp. 247–52.
21. Ibid., p. 251.
22. Ibid., p. 258.
23. Ibid., pp. 260–61.
24. Ibid., p. 262.

Chapter Twelve

1. Samuels, *Henry Adams: The Major Phase*, pp. 498–501.
2. *The Life of George Cabot Lodge* (Boston, 1911), pp. 9–13.
3. Ibid., p. 14.
4. Ibid., p. 9.
5. Ibid., p. 27.
6. Ibid., p. 45.
7. Ibid., p. 49.
8. Ibid., p. 61.
9. Ibid., p. 68.
10. Ibid., p. 109.
11. Ibid., p. 111.
12. Ibid., p. 118.
13. Ibid., p. 158.
14. Ibid., p. 174.
15. Ibid., pp. 175–80.
16. George Hochfield, *Henry Adams* (New York, 1962), p. 143.

Selected Bibliography

PRIMARY SOURCES

1. Books (in order of first publication)
Chapters of Erie, and Other Essays, by Charles F. Adams, Jr., and Henry Adams. Boston: James R. Osgood and Co., 1871.
The Life of Albert Gallatin. Philadelphia: J. B. Lippincott and Co., 1879.
Democracy: An American Novel. (Anonymous). New York: Henry Holt and Co., 1884.
John Randolph. Boston and New York: Houghton, Mifflin and Co., 1882.
Esther: A Novel. (Pseudonym, Frances Snow Compton). New York: Henry Holt and Co., 1884.
History of the United States of America During the First Administration of Thomas Jefferson, 1801–1805. Privately printed. Cambridge, Massachusetts: John Wilson and Son, 1884; revised edition: 2 vols., New York: Charles Scribner's Sons, 1889.
History of the United States of America During the Second Administration of Thomas Jefferson, 1805–1809. Privately printed. Cambridge, Massachusetts: John Wilson and Son, 1885; revised edition: 2 vols., New York: Charles Scribner's Sons, 1890.
History of the United States of America During the First Administration of James Madison, 1809–1813. Privately printed. Cambridge, Massachusetts: John Wilson and Son, 1888; revised edition: 2 vols., New York: Charles Scribner's Sons, 1890.
History of the United States of America During the Second Administration of James Madison, 1813–1817. 3 vols. New York: Charles Scribner's Sons, 1891.
Historical Essays. New York: Charles Scribner's Sons, 1891.
Memoirs of Marau Taaroa, Last Queen of Tahiti. Privately printed, 1893; revised edition: *Memoirs of Arii Taimai E.* Paris, 1901.
Mont-Saint-Michel and Chartres, with an introduction by Ralph Adams Cram. Boston: Houghton, Mifflin and Co., 1913; first printed privately and anonymously, Washington, 1904.
The Education of Henry Adams. Privately printed, Washington, 1907; reprinted, Boston and New York: Houghton Mifflin Co., 1918.
The Life of George Cabot Lodge. Boston and New York: Houghton Mifflin Co., 1911.

2. Edited Materials (in chronological order)

Essays in Anglo-Saxon Law. Boston: Little, Brown and Co., 1876.

Documents Relating to New-England Federalism, 1800–1815. Boston: Little, Brown and Co., 1877.

The Writings of Albert Gallatin. 3 vols. Philadelphia: J. B. Lippincott and Co., 1879.

Letters of John Hay and Extracts from Diary. 3 vols. Washington: privately printed by Clara Hay, 1908.

3. Selected Periodical Publications (in chronological order)

"Holden Chapel," *Harvard Magazine* 1 (1855), 210–15.

"My Old Room," *Harvard Magazine* 2 (1856), 290–97.

"Captain John Smith," *North American Review* 104 (1867), 1–30.

Review of Sir Charles Lyell's *Principles of Geology, North American Review* 107 (1868), 465–501.

"American Finance, 1865–1869," *Edinburgh Review* 129 (1869), 504–33.

"Civil Service Reform," *North American Review* 109 (1869), 443–75.

"The Session," *North American Review* III (1870), 29–62.

"The New York Gold Conspiracy," *Westminster Review* 94 (1870), 411–36.

"Harvard College," *North American Review* 114 (1872), 110–47.

"Freeman's *Historical Essays," North American Review* 114 (1872), 193–96.

"King's *Mountaineering in the Sierra Nevada," North American Review* 114 (1872), 445–48.

"Freeman's *History of the Norman Conquest," North American Review* 118 (1874), 176–81.

"Coulange's *Ancient City," North American Review* 118 (1874), 390–97.

"Sohm's *Procedure de la Lex Salica," North American Review* 118 (1874), 416–25.

"Stubbs' *Constitutional History of England," North American Review* 119 (1874), 233–44.

"Kitchin's *History of France," North American Review* 119 (1874), 442–47.

"Parkman's *Old Regime in Canada," North American Review* 120 (1875), 175–79.

"The Quincy Memoirs and Speeches," *North American Review* 120 (1875), 235–36.

"Bancroft's *History of the United States," North American Review* 120 (1875), 424–32.

"Maine's *Early History of Institutions," North American Review* 120 (1875), 432–38.

"Green's *Short History of the English People," North American Review* 121 (1875), 216–24.

Henry Adams and Henry Cabot Lodge. "Von Holst's *History of the United States," North American Review* 123 (1876), 328–61.

"Napoléon Ier et Saint-Domingue," *La Revue Historique* 24 (1884), 92–130.

"The Tendency of History." *Annual Report of the American Historical Association for the Year 1894*. Washington: Government Printing Office, 1895.

"The Great Secession Winter of 1860–61," *Proceedings of the Massachusetts Historical Society* 43 (1910), 656–89.

4. Letters and Collected Essays

A Cycle of Adams Letters, 1861–1865, ed. Worthington Chauncey Ford. 2 vols. Boston and New York: Houghton Mifflin Co., 1920.

Charles Vandersee, ed. "Henry Adams' Education of Martha Cameron: Letters, 1888–1916." *Texas Studies in Literature and Language* 10 (1968), 233–93.

Henry Adams and his Friends, ed. Harold Dean Cater. Boston: Houghton Mifflin Co., 1947.

Letters of Henry Adams (1858–1891), ed. Worthington Chauncey Ford. Boston and New York: Houghton Mifflin Co., 1930.

Letters of Henry Adams (1892–1918), ed. Worthington Chauncey Ford. Boston and New York: Houghton Mifflin Co., 1938.

Letters to a Niece and Prayer to the Virgin of Chartres, with a Niece's Memories, ed. Mabel La Farge. Boston and New York: Houghton Mifflin Co., 1920.

The Degradation of the Democratic Dogma, with an introduction by Brooks Adams. New York: Macmillan, 1919.

SECONDARY SOURCES

ADAMS, BROOKS. "The Heritage of Henry Adams." *The Degradation of the Democratic Dogma*. New York: Macmillan, 1919. Adulatory. Interprets Henry's philosophy as a continuation of that of John Quincy Adams.

ADAMS, JAMES TRUSLOW. *The Adams Family*. Boston: Little, Brown and Co., 1931. History beginning with John Adams and continuing through the generation of Henry Adams.

———. *Henry Adams*. New York: Albert and Charles Boni, Inc., 1933. Popular biography.

ADAMS, MARIAN HOOPER. *Letters of Mrs. Henry Adams, 1865–1883*, ed. Ward Thoron. Boston: Little, Brown and Co., 1936. Lively record of travels and social life in Washington.

AUCHINCLOSS, LOUIS. *Henry Adams*. Minneapolis: University of Minnesota Press, 1971 (UMPAW, no. 93). Believes that "Prayer to the Virgin of Chartres" synthesizes Adams's philosophy.

BARBER, DAVID S. "Henry Adams' *Esther*: the Nature of Individuality and Immortality." *New England Quarterly* 45 (1972), 227–40. Finds that *Esther*'s actions at the end of the novel are necessary to preserve her individuality.

BAYM, MAX I. *The French Education of Henry Adams.* New York: Columbia University Press, 1951. Demonstrates that Adams derived much of his thought and technique from French sources.

BLACKMUR, R. P. *The Expense of Greatness.* New York: Arrow Editions, 1940. Believes that Adams carried the principle of unity to the point of failure, where it shows most value.

———. "The Harmony of True Liberalism: Henry Adams' *Mont-Saint-Michel and Chartres.*" *Sewanee Review* 60 (1952) 1–27. Stresses Adams's artistry.

———. "The Novels of Henry Adams." *Sewanee Review* 51 (1943), 281–304. Suggests that the facts of Adams's life help to illuminate his novels.

CAIRNS, JOHN C. "The Successful Quest of Henry Adams." *South Atlantic Quarterly* 57 (1958), 168–93. Believes that Adams developed an understanding of the "relativity of all historical interpretation."

CAMPBELL, HARRY M. "Academic Criticism on Henry Adams: Confusion about Chaos." *Midcontinent American Studies Journal* 7 (1966), 7–14. Reviews criticism of Yvor Winters and Robert E. Spiller.

CARGILL, OSCAR. "The Medievalism of Henry Adams." *Essays and Studies in Honor of Carleton Brown.* New York: New York University Press, 1940, pp. 296–329. Finds that *Mont-Saint-Michel and Chartres* is a "prose poem rather than anything else."

CHANDLER, ALICE: *A Dream of Order: The Medieval Ideal in Nineteenth-Century English Literature.* Lincoln: University of Nebraska Press, 1970. Feels that in Adams "medievalism . . . becomes the grounds for the bleakest pessimism."

COLACURCIO, MICHAEL. "*Democracy* and *Esther:* Henry Adams' Flirtation with Pragmatism." *American Quarterly* 19 (1967), 53–70. Finds that Adams's novels show him tempted by pragmatism, which he does not espouse.

———. "The Dynamo and the Angelic Doctor: The Bias of Henry Adams' Medievalism." *American Quarterly* 17 (1965), 696–712. Suggests that *Chartres* represents that in the thought of Thomas Aquinas begins the chaos of the post-Darwinian world.

COMMAGER, HENRY STEELE. "Henry Adams." *Marcus W. Jernegan Essays in American Historiography.* Chicago: University of Chicago Press, 1937, pp. 191–206. Avers that "to the student of American history the contemplation of Adams is the beginning of wisdom."

———. *The American Mind.* New Haven: Yale University Press, 1950. Feels that Adams turned in desperation to the Virgin of Chartres as a symbol of unity.

CONDER, JOHN. *A Formula of his Own: Henry Adams's Literary Experiment.* Chicago: University of Chicago Press, 1970. Examines *Chartres* and the *Education* to show "thematic unity based on opposition between two cultures."

CROWLEY, JOHN W. "The Suicide of the Artist: Henry Adams' *Life of George Cabot Lodge.*" *New England Quarterly* 46 (1973), 189–204. Claims that the "*Life of Lodge* denies the shaping power of the imagination which Adams seems to affirm in the *Education.*"

DONOVAN, TIMOTHY P. *Henry Adams and Brooks Adams: The Education of Two American Historians.* Norman: University of Oklahoma Press, 1961. Believes that Adams sought "to justify the determinism of the nineteenth century."

GABRIEL, RALPH H. *The Course of American Democratic Thought.* New York: Ronald Press, 1940. Attributes to Adams the idea that "democratic faith is doomed."

GLICKSBERG, CHARLES I. "Henry Adams and the Aesthetic Quest." *Prairie Schooner* 25 (1951), 241–50. Suggests that *Chartres* and the *Education* show that the artist in Adams had emerged.

HARBERT, EARL N. *The Force So Much Closer Home: Henry Adams and the Adams Family.* New York: New York University Press, 1977. Discusses the Adams tradition and what Henry Adams made of his heritage.

HOCHFIELD, GEORGE. *Henry Adams: An Introduction and Interpretation.* New York: Barnes and Noble, 1962. Believes that "what Adams discovered was that life had no meaning."

HOLT, HENRY. *Garrulities of an Octogenarian Editor.* New York: Henry Holt and Co., 1923. Contains reminiscences about the publication of Adams's novels.

HUME, ROBERT. *Runaway Star: An Appreciation of Henry Adams.* Ithaca, New York: Cornell University Press, 1951. Finds Adams an instance of "the affirmed invincibility of the human spirit in the face of what must overwhelm it."

JORDY, WILLIAM H. *Henry Adams: Scientific Historian.* New Haven: Yale University Press, 1952. Emphasizes the "scientific" elements in Adams's writing of history.

JOSEPHSON, MATTHEW. *Portrait of the Artist as American.* New York: Harcourt Brace and Co., 1930. Finds the *Education* "the most tragic record of human frustration ever written by an American."

KARIEL, HENRY S. "The Limits of Social Science: Henry Adams' Quest for Order." *American Political Science Review* 50 (1956), 1074–92. Adams's quest stemmed from the failure of science and art to provide a basis for knowledge of man and society.

KORETZ, GENE H. "Augustine's *Confessions* and *The Education of Henry Adams.*" *Comparative Literature* 12 (1960), 193–206. Suggests that Adams saw in the *Confessions* a model which harmonized the aesthetic and the didactic.

KRAUS, MICHAEL. *The Writing of American History.* Norman: University of Oklahoma Press, 1953. Finds Adams a transitional figure between the literary and the scientific historians.

LEVENSON, J. C. *The Mind and Art of Henry Adams.* Boston: Houghton Mifflin Co., 1957. Believes that Adams, dissatisfied with his *History,* dwelt more and more on the negative aspects of life.

LYON, MELVIN. *Symbol and Idea in Henry Adams.* Lincoln: University of Nebraska Press, 1970. Suggests that "Adams' sensibility operates ultimately in terms of concepts."

MANE, ROBERT. *Henry Adams on the Road to Chartres.* Cambridge, Massachusetts: Harvard University Press, 1971. Avers that "the unity of the Middle Ages which Adams struggles to recapture is a unity of perception."

MAUD, RALPH. "Henry Adams: Irony and Impasse." *Essays in Criticism* 8 (1958), 381–92. Believes that investigation of Adams's irony will only confirm the despair he felt.

MCINTYRE, JOHN P. "Henry Adams and the Unity of Chartres." *Twentieth Century Literature* 7 (1962), 159–71. Finds that Adams's Thomistic cathedral is imaginative rather than philosophically correct.

MINDEL, JOSEPH. "The Uses of Metaphor: Henry Adams and the Symbols of Science." *Journal of the History of Ideas* 27 (1965), 89–102. Emphasized that Adams stressed "the metaphoric link between history and science."

MUNFORD, HOWARD M. "Henry Adams: The Limitations of Science." *Southern Review* 4 (1968), 59–71. Asserts that the Dynamic Theory of History would make for a more humane society than science.

MURRAY, JAMES G. *Henry Adams.* New York: Twayne Publishers, 1974. Believes Adams was a transcendentalist who became an existentialist.

NUHN, FERNER. *The Wind Blew from the East: A Study in the Orientation of American Culture.* New York: Harper and Brothers, 1942. Interprets Adams as an "hereditary aristocrat in a democratic world."

PETERSON, MERRILL D. "Henry Adams on Jefferson the President." *Virginia Quarterly Review* 39 (1963), 187–201. Finds Adams's portrait of Jefferson deficient, but no alternative is yet available.

ROELOFS, GERRIT H. "Henry Adams: Pessimism and the Intelligent Use of Doom." *ELH: A Journal of Literary History* 17 (1950), 214–39. Believes that the Henry Adams of the *Education* is only a masque.

RULE, HENRY B. "Henry Adams' Satire on Human Intelligence: Its Method and Purpose." *Centennial Review* 15 (1971), 430–44. Suggests that Adams dramatizes the need of the Western world for greater mind power.

SAMUELS, ERNEST. "Henry Adams and the Gossip Mills." *Essays in American and English Literature Presented to Bruce Robert McElderry, Jr.* Ed. Max F. Schulz et al. Athens, Ohio: University of Ohio Press, 1967, pp. 59–75. Discusses the relationship of Adams and Elizabeth Cameron.

————. *The Young Henry Adams.* Cambridge, Massachusetts: Harvard University Press, 1948. *Henry Adams: The Middle Years.* Cambridge, Massachusetts: Harvard University Press, 1958. *Henry Adams: The Major Phase.* Cambridge, Massachusetts: Harvard University Press, 1964. The three volumes constitute an enormously detailed biography. Definitive.

SCHEYER, ERNST. *The Circle of Henry Adams: Art and Artists.* Detroit: Wayne State University Press, 1970. Stresses Adams's interest in the visual arts.

SCHMITZ, NEIL. "The Difficult Art of American Political Fiction: Henry Adams' *Democracy* as Tragical Satire." *Western Humanities Review* 25 (1971), 147–62. Suggests that "by excising morality from politics, Adams dismantled nineteenth-century liberalism."

SHAW, PETER. "Blood is Thicker than Irony: Henry Adams' *History.*" *New England Quarterly* 40 (1967), 163–87. Finds that Adams's *History* methodically discredits the Adams family's opponents.

SPILLER, ROBERT E. "Henry Adams." *Literary History of the United States.* Ed. R. E. Spiller et al. New York: The Macmillan Co., 1948, pp. 1080–1103. Finds that Adams changes from a man of thought to a man of emotion.

STEVENSON, ELIZABETH. *Henry Adams: A Biography.* New York: The Macmillan Co., 1955. Explains that "Adams' gift and his flaw was pride."

VANDERSEE, CHARLES. "The Hamlet in Henry Adams." *Shakespeare Survey* 24 (1971), 87–104. Points out that Adams portrays himself in the *Education* as a Hamlet.

————. "Henry Adams (1838–1918)." *American Literary Realism* 2 (1969), 89–119. Bibliography.

WAGNER, VERN. *The Suspension of Henry Adams.* Detroit: Wayne State University Press, 1969. Believes that the explanation of Adams is to be found in an examination of his style.

WASSER, HENRY. *The Scientific Thought of Henry Adams.* Thessaloniki, Greece: University of Salonika Press, 1956. Explains that proof of the rightness or wrongness of Adams's speculations about entropy awaits a decision by scientists as to whether the universe is closed or open.

WHITE, LYNN, JR. "Dynamo and Virgin Reconsidered." *American Scholar* 27 (1958), 183–94. Suggests that the chief glory of the Middle Ages was not in its art and thought, as Adams believed, but in its use of nonhuman power.

WINTERS, YVOR. "Henry Adams, or the Creation of Confusion." *The Anatomy of Nonsense.* Norfolk, Connecticut: New Directions, 1943, pp. 23–87. Avers that Adams's *History* "is penetrated with precise intelligence," but that his later books show "the disintegration of a mind."

WISH, HARVEY. *The American Historian: A Social-Intellectual History of the Writing of the American Past.* New York: Oxford University Press, 1960. Believes that Adams "contemplated power politics without mysticism but with flashes of historical insight into the future."

WRIGHT, NATHALIA. "Henry Adams's Theory of History: A Puritan Defense." *New England Quarterly* 18 (1945), 204–10. Finds Adams's theory of history not worthy of his brilliant faculties.

Index